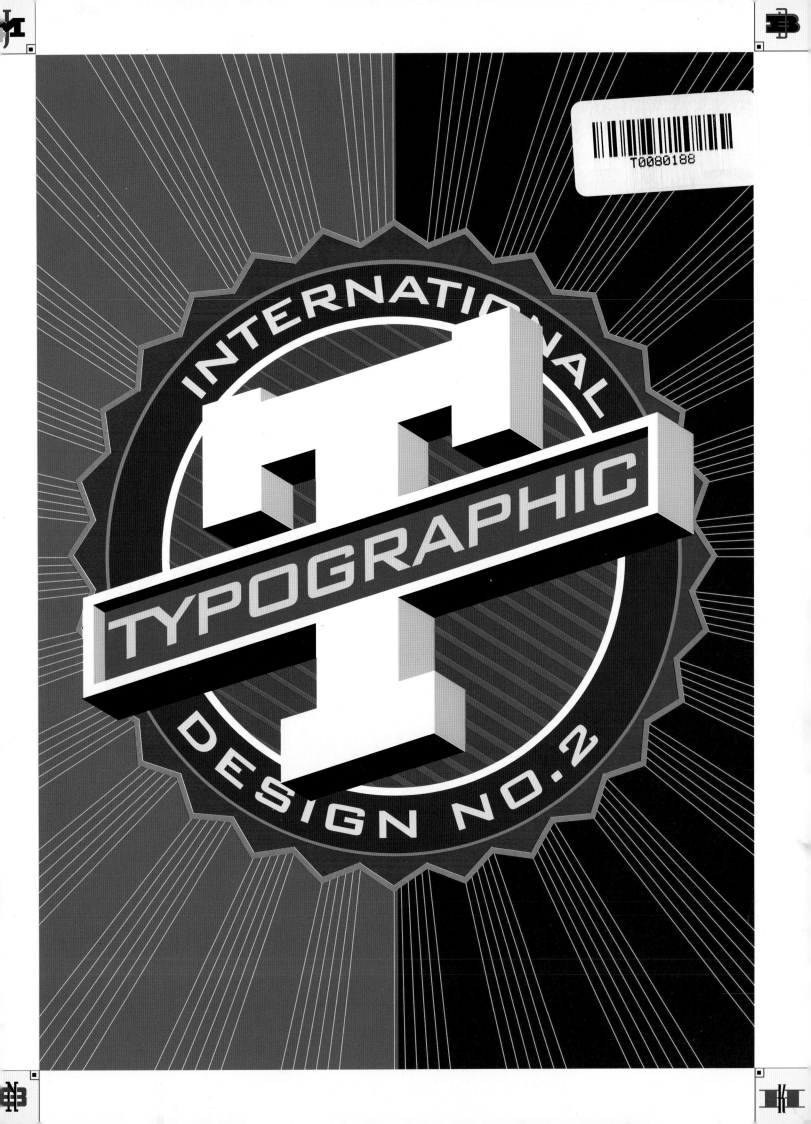

INTERNATIONAL

TYPOGRAPHIC

DESIGN NO.2

## PRODUCTION CREDITS

*Designer: David Brier*

*Production & Typography: Kim Plosia*

*Cover Art Production: Bob Hansen*

*Administrative Associates:*
*Joelle Pastor*
*Hope Wenzel*
*Kim Plosia*
*Alexis Posyton*

*Color Photography:*
*Manny Akis*

*The text in this volume is set in Adobe Garamond Italic, Bank Gothic, Modula Serif and Mekanik.*

*Library of Congress Catalog Card Number 94-076991*

*Distributors to the trade in the United States and Canada:*
*Van Nostrand Reinhold*
*115 Fifth Avenue*
*New York, NY 10003*

*Distributed throughout the rest of the world by:*
*Hearst Books International*
*1350 Avenue of the Americas*
*New York, NY 10019*

*Publisher:*
*Madison Square Press*
*10 East 23rd Street*
*New York, NY 10010*

*Printed in Hong Kong*

## ACKNOWLEDGEMENTS

*The following are acknowledged for their selfless assistance and persistence,*
*which made this project possible:*

| | |
|---|---|
| *Neville Brody* | *Joelle Pastor* |
| *Jo Cincotta* | *Kim Plosia* |
| *Kent Hunter* | *Alexis Posyton* |
| *Jerry McConnell* | *Hope Wenzel* |
| *Minora Morita* | *Drucker Printing* |
| *Jennifer Morla* | *Fox River Paper* |

*My deepest thanks also go to the many other individuals*
*who provided support along the way and, without whom,*
*this volume would not exist.*

## DEDICATION

*This continuation of this series is made possible only by the continued standard of performance*
*of our peers. In this industry of visual communicators, we shape how others see the world.*
*It is with this responsibility and care that this book is here.*

*David Brier*
*1994*

# CONTENTS

CLOCKWISE FROM TOP: *Neville Brody's scalp, Neville Brody's left ear, Neville Brody's cleft, Neville Brody's right cheek*

*The following conversation between Neville Brody, David Brier*

*and Joelle Pastor (who was the silent partner in this conversation)*

*occurred at the ATypI Conference in Antwerp, Belgium*

*in November 1993.*

SO NEVILLE, LET'S TALK TYPE.

*Where to start. Today there are no standards anymore and there shouldn't be any standards. At least not until things settle down, because at the moment, anything is possible. And there should be no rules because language and communication is changing so dramatically, and now is the time to explore and experiment as much as possible. One must try to find new ways of dealing with the new world and things in it.*

WHAT ARE YOUR VIEWS ON "THE DESKTOP REVOLUTION"?

*My feeling is that desktop publishing is like a camera. The camera gave to everyone the ability to record social reality. Why not? It just reformed everything, and took away the artist's main substance which was to record social reality. They were skilled; they were the only people who could do this. And what's happening in design is the same. Now with desktop publishing, you don't need as many designers as you once did because big companies go in-house. What a designer does today is give you a template in a system, set you up and then it's in-house. With desktop publishing you don't need the daily contact with the designer. Like the camera, you have everyone using cameras but you still have great photographers.*

## IS TODAY'S DESIGNER EXPENDABLE?

*There is still going to be a need for great designers or great communicators, but the challenge before us is changing totally. It's a shift away from production – the big change is from print production to electronic communication and no one knows what the hell that's going to look like! It's 500 lanes of a super-information highway and if you don't know which way to look you're going to get run over. It's a big challenge for designers to get a hold of that and develop the language to be used.*

*The point is the design profession has become so sullen and so complacent in its little throne, its little glass house, that it hasn't really realized that the world has moved on and changed. It still somehow thinks this industry is still a protected profession. Reality is gone for certain people which I shouldn't name. I still feel that graphic design or the design industry is an elite industry – a monastic, elite industry. I forgot that design is habit forming. So David, what are you working on?*

## WELL, IF YOU MUST KNOW...OH, I'M SORRY NEVILLE, CARRY ON.

*I think the same thing has happened in design that happened in art...when the camera came along, the artist was "redundant." It forced artists to go through a lengthy period of self examination and self justification, "Why art?" And the same process has already started in design.*

## WHAT ABOUT TYPE IN DESIGN?

*Design has no alternative but, for the moment, to examine its very role – what the fuck is it doing? And the concept of good and bad design is gone. There is no criteria. How the hell can you say this is a good piece of typography? All you can say is this is a beautiful or an ugly piece of typography. That's it!*

*Typography for me today is a more extinct concept. What you have to talk about is language and you'll find that with digital information, this becomes a more and more expressive vehicle. Language* will evolve more towards pictograms or usable expression forms. I mean a good example is in art. If you take someone like Paul Klee or Kandinsky, they are like a mirror. It became more like an abstractive language. The more flexible it is, the more successful it will be in its role of reflecting what's happening in society, social change. Art had that role. You could look at where we are and say this is a mirror of social undercurrent. The same is happening in design. Now its been liberated from the straight jacket of having to control information the way it used to. It's been liberated from all the judgment of long ago, now design is being split into two parts. First, you still need designers, you still need someone to give people systems. Once that is over, you have the other role, which is art. It becomes a free form of expression. With digital communication, it's like a painting where paint doesn't dry. The paint is digital media. It's always fluid. It's always changing and that's what we're trying to head toward. This branches into new areas and a new platform for design and type.

This is the most exciting time ever to be involved with type design. It's the biggest change we can ever imagine possibly happening. Now and then, I meet designers and, shit, they try and hold up the design profession as being this untouchable precious little club and it actually offends me.

WHERE DO YOU SEE THE FUTURE GOING FOR TYPOGRAPHY?

We've given a name to the new typography which is Freeform Typography. It's where the typographic languages are liberated from having to do with words which is a strange thing for people to comprehend. It is actually a new form of communication that the keyboard becomes a paint pattern. And when you look at a piece of text you can look at the words or you actually recognize other things out of the text.

The certain rhythms, patterns, the coloring and the shape of the letters give you a whole other emotional response. What we're trying to do is liberate typography form from words. We are trying to say that there is an actual emotional response to the visual within written communications.

CLOCKWISE FROM TOP LEFT: *Neville Brody, David Brier, Jennifer Morla and Kent Hunter*

*Neville Brody currently runs his own studio in London, working with many international clients in many countries. Brody's studio works with corporate, fashion, music and media companies. The scope of his work is broad, encompassing magazine redesign, record covers, three-dimensional design and the formation of FontShop International, a network of computer typeface supply sources, that develops and publishes its own fonts. In April 1988, the Victoria and Albert Museum in London hosted Brody's major retrospective.*

DAVID BRIER, PRESIDENT AND CREATIVE DIRECTOR OF DBD INTERNATIONAL, LTD., IS A SELF-TAUGHT DESIGNER AND TYPOGRAPHER. HE HAS AN IMPRESSIVE LIST OF CLIENTS INCLUDING AT&T, GRP RECORDS, ESTEÉ LAUDER AND CONTINENTAL INSURANCE TO NAME A FEW. IN ADDITION TO BEING PUBLISHED IN A HOST OF PROFESSIONAL MAGAZINES, HE HAS ALSO DESIGNED A NUMBER OF NATIONAL MAGAZINE COVERS. HE ALSO PUBLISHES THE AWARD-WINNING "GRAPHIC RELIEF, A QUARTERLY INDULGENCE."

Kent Hunter is Executive Design Director and a principal of Frankfurt Balkind Partners, an integrated communications agency based in New York, Los Angeles, and San Francisco. He directs a team of designers on assignments that include annual reports, identity programs, magazines, posters and multi-media presentations. Kent is a past vice-president of the New York chapter of the AIGA. He has judged numerous design shows and frequently lectures around the country.

Jennifer Morla is President and Creative Director of Morla Design, Inc. She has been honored internationally for her ability to pair wit and elegance on everything from annual reports to music videos. She has been featured in numerous national and international magazines. Ms. Morla has been the recipient of the Marget Larsen Award for Designer of the Year and was declared one of the Fifteen Masters of Design by *How* magazine. In addition to teaching Senior Graphic Design at California College of Arts and Crafts, she paints, sculpts, creates site-specific installations and is a featured speaker and frequent national show juror.

# COMMENTARY

THE FOLLOWING IS FROM A DISCUSSION ON THE CURRENT STATE OF TYPOGRAPHY AND THE EFFECT OF TECHNOLOGY ON THIS GRAPHIC ELEMENT. THIS ROUNDTABLE DISCUSSION OCCURRED JUST OUTSIDE OF NEW YORK CITY ON SATURDAY, SEPTEMBER 11, 1993 WITH NEVILLE BRODY OF LONDON, JENNIFER MORLA OF SAN FRANCISCO, KENT HUNTER OF NEW YORK AND DAVID BRIER OF NEW JERSEY DURING THE JUDGING FOR THE PIECES TO BE INCLUDED IN THIS BOOK.

WITH DIGITAL TECHNOLOGY AND THE COMPUTER INFLUENCING THE DIRECTION OF TYPE AND DESIGN, WHAT COMMENTS DO YOU HAVE – POSITIVE OR NEGATIVE – REGARDING TYPE TRENDS AND THE CHANGES YOU SEE TODAY?

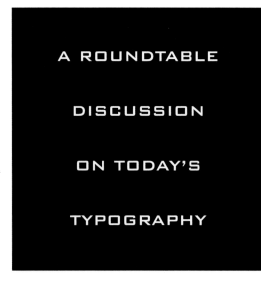

A ROUNDTABLE

DISCUSSION

ON TODAY'S

TYPOGRAPHY

**JM:** *I don't think a value judgment is appropriate. During the past decade, typography has neither improved nor degenerated, it has evolved. The Mac has changed and will continue to change typography more than we can imagine. Certainly there is a definite "transparency" with the increased use of the computer. At the same time, there is a classicism that people are also coming back to.*

**NB:** *As Kent said yesterday, the digital technology is something everyone will have to turn to design typefaces. It actually allows much more personal access to communication – 8,000 fonts this year...6,000 fonts last year. In three years, there will be 20,000 different fonts. Just look at any digital font catalog to see its growing very rapidly.*

**DB:** *I agree with Neville. The opportunity for personalization is enormous. After all, a major tool is now in the hands of everyone. My only concern is with the uneducated notion that "a computer equals design ability." For many purists, the broad use of the computer as a type tool by non-artisans is the death of type; for others, it opens up a whole new world. Unfortunately, the knowledge of type doesn't come on disk as well.*

**KH:** *I agree with everything said, yet I see an even more personalized and customized approach to fonts. One can certainly create one's own, of course. Additionally, I see quite an array of modifications of type available and, in logo design creation especially, you can really go all out. It's amazing that what can now be done on the Mac so quickly used to take so long. Obviously, the computer is only a tool that's been put in our hands, so it becomes so simple to modify a typeface, make something heavier or even customize a rule.*

*This year, an illustrator gave us an alphabet in his painting. We liked it so much that we had him do this alphabet for us. We then digitized it and that became our font for the book. So its pretty nice to have the opportunity to swiftly do a custom font for an annual report.*

WHAT ARE YOUR VIEWS ON DIGITAL TYPE OPPORTUNI-
TIES, ON PROGRAMS AND ON TRENDS THAT AFFECT
THE DESIGN PROCESS?

**NB:** *Our office policy: if it moves, digitize it. Today, most*

*type designers often don't sketch – they go straight to the Mac. That is a notable change that should be welcome.*

**DB:** *In terms of technology, I see differences in the direction of design, because type and type programs are in the hands of **anyone and everyone**. The whole specialized field of typography used to be in the hands of the people who were ideally trained as artisans in the field of typography. Now it is in the hands of designers, most of whom have no formal training in the area.*

*There's a lot of experimentation going on with a lot of things that are making it to press that never would have made it before. Sometimes good things are coming out of it. There are some very bad things coming out of it by which I mean inappropriate and non-communicative solutions. A big metamorphosis is going on that is not going to settle for a while, but it is opening new doors and is interesting.*

WHAT DO YOU THINK OF TYPE STANDARDS TAUGHT IN SCHOOL THAT WILL AFFECT THE NEXT GENERATION OF DESIGNERS? DO YOU THINK STANDARDS WILL BE MAINTAINED?

**NB:** *There is no such thing as good typography. There's only appropriate typography and the ability to choose the right language for the right content.*

**JM:** *It's still an issue of understanding that the total language itself is something any designer can and should refer to. I think that there is less of a historic understanding of type. I was trained in a very traditional typographic background. With the Mac, you go through a type library – you never see the typefaces – all you see are the names of these typefaces. So there was a time when you would go through a type book and you would literally see the alphabet and the entire font. Now unless the student is familiar with every single font on the Mac, they are only going to be drawn to the ones they have used before. This is* *not necessarily absolute — there are those that break the rules — but it's that you don't have a complete quick visual reference.*

**KH:** *It's a problem we can't keep up. Our technology guys in-house have to consistently update our reference books, and there is no way we can keep up. I've always liked looking over designers shoulders, they'll see new fonts and scan them. It's amazing the things that pop up on each person's computer because of what they've seen. It's almost like...font of the week. It's sometimes even font of the day. You do go through love affairs with fonts.*

**DB:** *I have a more traditional view, I personally would have a designer do stuff by hand and really do comps by hand for a while before I would have him get on the computer. I feel that new designers are given such a humongous tool and such room and leverage, without a balance of knowledge to maximize the tool. Additionally, the computer easily becomes the crutch that dictates — because of program limitations and existing font libraries already on the system — certain design patterns. At that point, the designer forfeits his or her initiative and freedom of vision. I have a traditional background very much like Jennifer's. She's got a traditional foundation from which to depart — that's my tendency as well.*

## WHERE DO YOU THINK STYLES ARE GOING?

**NB:** *Style today is almost irrelevant.*

**JM:** *Style is simply a matter of evolution.*

**KH:** *There's nothing that predominant.*

**NB:** *Design is totally deconstructive in its current form.*

**JM:** *It still has to do with what's appropriate, the editorial that accompanies visuals and the audience that you're talking to.*

**DB:** *Stylewise, I see a lot more plagiarism these days than I have seen in the past.*

**KH:** *That's a different issue.*

**DB:** *Yes it is separate, but quite relevant, because the next hot designer, or the next hot magazine, is going to be the next hot trend for the next 12 months.*

**JM:** *Typefaces become an accepted vernacular of the populace a lot faster than what you think. When Helvetica was designed, it was not considered a legible typeface nor used as body copy. Yet, within 20 years, it is a defacto face for any sort of modern text book or annual report. The 60's and the 70's were all Helvetica – so we are adaptable. What today may seem somewhat indiscernible can influence a change in our visual language. In order to accommodate that, I put my designers on the Mac right away. I might provide a sketch, but there is no in-between with them. The knowledge of the computer is what allows them to push it and come up with ideas. Ideas are the most important element but the computer and the software involved gives you those ideas also.*

**WHAT IS YOUR CONCEPT OF THE COMPUTER?**

**NB:** *Tradition changes. You can't teach something from ten years ago as being valid now. So it is with these kids that are playing Nintendo from whatever age – it's second nature to utilize a computer and they wouldn't imagine any other way of doing it.*

**KH:** *Computers allow for a lot more mediocrity.*

**NB:** *That's the mistake! Mediocrity is actually what would have been shit before but is now reaching mediocrity.*

**KH:** *It's "passable design" and they certainly buy Neville's fonts and do something that looks good because it's a nice font rather than good design being there or a good concept being there. I would like to think the higher end is more visible now because there's so much in the middle.*

**DB:** *The truth is the pencil didn't require years of training or familiarity. One either had talent or one didn't. The profession is getting confused between a) an individual's ability to use a program with literacy and skill and b) his native talent. One couldn't hide behind a pencil. Today, one can hide behind a computer and a program. Computers only magnify the symptoms. In the hands of a truly talented designer, it is a marvelous tool.*

**NB:** *And the criticism here is it's making it easy to sit on the Mac and produce something that looks good without having a single idea.*

**DB:** *Exactly.*

**JM:** *Well, there's also the immediacy to it. You know back in traditional typesetting, you'd get a job set five different ways and review the options. It's so quick now and the print out is so quick that perhaps one doesn't go through all the stages of examination. The key issue is if the inquiry was done – that's what's important.*

## HOW DO YOU SEE THE ROLE OF THE SERVICE BUREAU? ARE CLIENT DEMANDS CHANGING?

**KH:** *Two years ago, we weren't doing anything completely electronic. Today, it's a whole new world. It's certainly changed the end process. It puts a lot more burden on us as designers. To take on the responsibilities of the typesetter was a huge change because you are responsible for proofreading and correction. A typo in a project is now something you're liable for – not the typesetter. We just took it for granted that it was proofread and it was professional. It's a huge enormous problem for us because we really are responsible for everything being corrected, regardless of the volume of generations of changes. We've had enormous problems with the work going to printers and the big problem is that printers are all at different points on the learning curve.*

**NB:** *What we want are good pre-press bureaus. We as designers are expected now to know about trapping needs to be done manually on the computer. If we sit down and do that stuff, we spend more time doing that than the actual job itself. They should know it but don't. We shouldn't have to do it.*

**DB:** *They should be aware of the ramifications. Their role is so much more comprehensive and affects the ultimate success of a piece that a real redefining of our industry's functions should be offered and applied on a global scale.*

**NB:** *Clients seem to expect this as part of the service now. You don't actually charge double.*

**KH:** *Clients aren't willing to pay for it – that's for sure. And printers aren't charging a lot less.*

**NB:** *We tried to charge computer time as extra and it sort of worked for a time because everyone does it and doesn't charge for it.*

**KH:** *Yeah, clients think tech time should be free as part of the design. We have a department that does the final mechanical on the computer and sends it out. And yes, those people cost money...and yes, that equipment costs money...and yes, that art department costs money. And we have to justify it constantly.*

**JM:** *In our office, that's a separate line item. It's not really a problem for us as we just have one fee in the office and it's always sort of the same. But then again we don't do the volume of annual reports that a firm like Kent's works on, where it would make a very big difference with what we do. Internally I know what part is typesetting or what part is "design" on the computer, but it's a very grey area nonetheless. I come to the computer different times during the project and I will switch everything around.*

**KH:** *Everyone loves when we do that, right? Especially at the last minute.*

**JM:** *At the last minute. That's what you were saying prepress gave you more time and flexibility for.*

HAVING VIEWED THE TRENDS OF WORK, WHAT IS YOUR VIEW OF THE DESIGN EFFORTS BEING MADE TODAY?

NB: *The majority of stuff I see is mediocre. So far, we are about half way through, and there's about 15 to 16 things I think are great, of which 2 or 3 are really inspiring.*

JM: *Whenever you take something to an extreme usually it's going to want more attention and so I can be just as astounded by an amazing clarity of simplicity as I would be by a very dense layering of deconstructed type. I think the problem I usually have viewing work is the stuff that falls in the middle ground where sort of a determination hadn't been made. The idea hadn't been there so it's sort of hazy and takes a little from here and a little from there and there's no singular vision.*

KH: *Well I agree with Jennifer about the things that really stood out and it's been one extreme to the other. The very shockingly simple were beautiful and really worked. On the other hand, I think these other entries were very complex — a lot of effort went into the typography and the concept, yet they've also restrained themselves. The problem we're having is the excess. The trick is always knowing when to stop — knowing when it's enough.*

NB: *Those are the dangers we noticed. It seems to be that the more different papers, inks and techniques would be used, the less substantial. In fact, the more the vellum, the more transparent the idea.*

DB: *I agree. There are a number of circumstances where a little germ of an idea would start with a spark and then die out. It was like Jennifer said, the singular idea is paramount. There are very few pieces that show an idea that is not deconstructed. The conviction of "Yes! This is what we're doing!" and carrying forth to really make the whole project a masterpiece regardless of style.*

DB: *By the way Neville, when is your birthday?*

NB: *Once a year. You David?*

DB: *Same. I knew we had a lot in common but this is too much.*

KH: *Hmm.*

# C

## CORPORATE

## IDENTITY

1    DESIGN FIRM: *Muller & Company*    DESIGNER: *Chris Muller*    LETTERER: *Chris Muller*    HEADLINE TYPEFACE: *Handlettering*    CLIENT: *Chris Muller*

2    DESIGN FIRM: *Sayles Graphic Design*    DESIGNER: *John Sayles*    LETTERER: *John Sayles*    HEADLINE TYPEFACE: *Handlettering*    CLIENT: *National Travelers Life*

3    DESIGN FIRM: *Sayles Graphic Design*    DESIGNER: *John Sayles*    LETTERER: *John Sayles*    HEADLINE TYPEFACE: *Handlettering*    CLIENT: *Adam Katzman*

4    DESIGN FIRM: *Rigsby Design, Inc.*    DESIGNER: *Lana Rigsby and Michael Thede*    HEADLINE TYPEFACE: *Futura Book*    TEXT TYPEFACE: *Copperplate*    CLIENT: *Bloodstone Pictures*

**5**

**6**

**7**

5  **DESIGN FIRM:** Zimmermann Crowe Design    **DESIGNER:** Neal Zimmermann    **LETTERER:** Alan Disparte    **HEADLINE TYPEFACE:** Handlettering    **CLIENT:** Levi Strauss & Co.

6  **DESIGN FIRM:** Lorna Stovall Design    **DESIGNER:** Lorna Stovall    **LETTERER:** Lorna Stovall    **HEADLINE TYPEFACE:** Handlettering    **CLIENT:** Capitol Records

7  **DESIGN FIRM:** Graphics & Designing Inc.    **DESIGNER:** Toshihiro Onimaru    **LETTERER:** Toshihiro Onimaru    **HEADLINE TYPEFACE:** Handlettering    **CLIENT:** Elan Co., Ltd.

# ACTIVE VOICE

8　DESIGN FIRM: *Hornall Anderson Design Works*　DESIGNER: *Jack Anderson, Julia LaPine, David Bates, Mary Hermes and Lian Ng*　HEADLINE TYPEFACE: *Futura*　CLIENT: *Active Voice*

9　DESIGN FIRM: *Ryle Smith Studio*　DESIGNER: *Ryle Smith*　LETTERER: *Ryle Smith*　HEADLINE TYPEFACE: *Handlettering*　CLIENT: *The Diner Theatre*

10　DESIGN FIRM: *Hornall Anderson Design Works*　DESIGNER: *Jack Anderson, Mary Hermes and David Bates*　LETTERER: *George Tanagi*　HEADLINE TYPEFACE: *Handlettering*　CLIENT: *Eaglemoor*

11  **DESIGN FIRM:** *Graphics & Designing Inc.*   **DESIGNER:** *Hiroyuki Hayashi*   **LETTERER:** *Hiroyuki Hayashi*   **HEADLINE TYPEFACE:** *Handlettering*   **CLIENT:** *Maze World Inc.*

12  **DESIGN FIRM:** *Graphics & Designing Inc.*   **DESIGNER:** *Toshihiro Onimaru*   **LETTERER:** *Toshihiro Onimaru*   **HEADLINE TYPEFACE:** *Handlettering*   **CLIENT:** *Unix Corporation*

13  **DESIGN FIRM:** *Michael Schwab Design*   **DESIGNER:** *Michael Schwab*   **LETTERER:** *Michael Schwab*   **HEADLINE TYPEFACE:** *Plakastil/Poster Style*   **CLIENT:** *Patrico Sinare*

14 **DESIGN FIRM:** *SullivanPerkins*     **DESIGNER:** *Lorraine Charman*     **LETTERER:** *Lorraine Charman*     **HEADLINE TYPEFACE:** *Modified Bureau Agency*     **TEXT TYPEFACE:** *Copperplate*     **CLIENT:** *The Rouse Co.*

15 **DESIGN FIRM:** *Hornall Anderson Design Works*     **DESIGNER:** *Jack Anderson, David Bates, Leo Raymundo and Lian Ng*     **HEADLINE TYPEFACE:** *Futura and Gill Sans*     **CLIENT:** *Giro Sports Design, Inc.*

16 **DESIGN FIRM:** *Abrams Design Group*     **DESIGNER:** *Denise Vorhees*     **LETTERER:** *Denise Vorhees*     **HEADLINE TYPEFACE:** *Futura Condensed*     **CLIENT:** *Forte Software, Inc.*

17 **DESIGN FIRM:** *Jager DiPaola Kemp Design*     **DESIGNER:** *Giovanna Jager*     **LETTERER:** *Giovanna Jager*     **HEADLINE TYPEFACE:** *Handlettering*     **CLIENT:** *Autumn Harp*

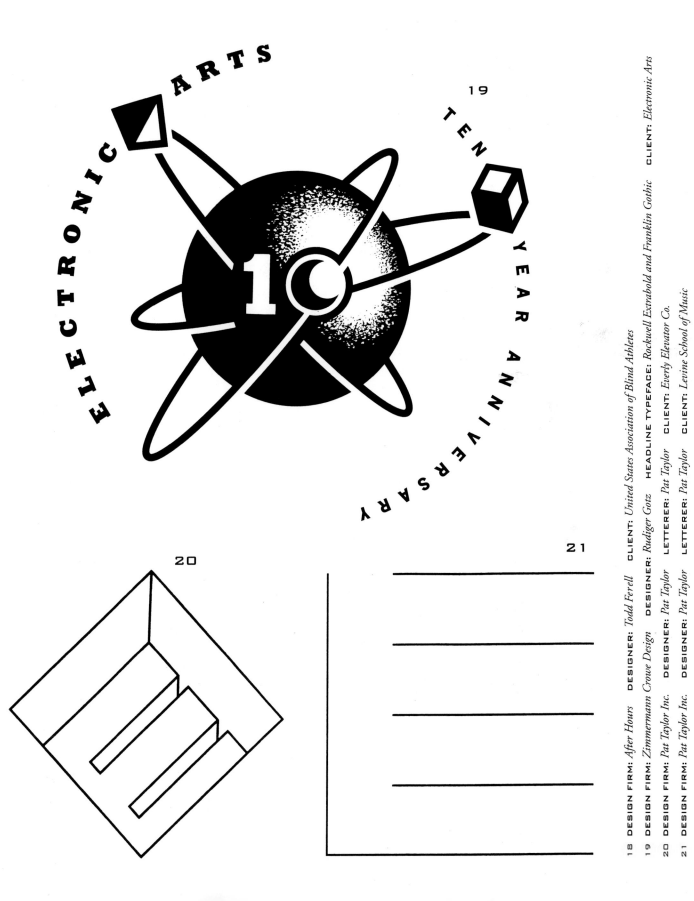

18  **DESIGN FIRM:** *After Hours*   **DESIGNER:** *Todd Ferell*   **CLIENT:** *United States Association of Blind Athletes*

19  **DESIGN FIRM:** *Zimmermann Crowe Design*   **DESIGNER:** *Rudiger Gotz*   **HEADLINE TYPEFACE:** *Rockwell Extrabold and Franklin Gothic*   **CLIENT:** *Electronic Arts*

20  **DESIGN FIRM:** *Pat Taylor Inc.*   **DESIGNER:** *Pat Taylor*   **LETTERER:** *Pat Taylor*   **CLIENT:** *Everly Elevator Co.*

21  **DESIGN FIRM:** *Pat Taylor Inc.*   **DESIGNER:** *Pat Taylor*   **LETTERER:** *Pat Taylor*   **CLIENT:** *Levine School of Music*

ELECTRONIC ARTS CELEBRATES IT'S TEN YEAR **ANNIVERSARY** OF CREATIVELY PLAYING **AROUND**

23

10 E | A

26

STEVE KEMMERLING

PHOTOGRAPHY

27

24

25

23  **DESIGN FIRM:** Zimmermann Crowe Design  **DESIGNER:** Rudiger Gotz  **HEADLINE TYPEFACE:** Bank Gothic and Franklin Gothic  **CLIENT:** Electronic Arts

24  **DESIGN FIRM:** Frank D'Astolfo Design  **DESIGNER:** Frank D'Astolfo  **LETTERER:** Frank D'Astolfo  **CLIENT:** XYZ Productions  **HEADLINE TYPEFACE:** Futura  **CLIENT:** California Cut Flower Commission

25  **DESIGN FIRM:** Vaxworks  **DESIGNER:** Joseph Vax and May Key Lee  **LETTERER:** Dug Waggoner  **CLIENT:** Carol Fantelli/Francesca Glass

26  **DESIGN FIRM:** Dale Design  **DESIGNER:** Jeffrey S. Dale  **HEADLINE TYPEFACE:** Futura  **CLIENT:** Steve Kemmerling Photography

27  **DESIGN FIRM:** Brad Norr Design  **DESIGNER:** Brad Norr  **HEADLINE TYPEFACE:** Univers

**28** MISOHAPI

**29** AUTUMN HARP

**31**

28 DESIGN FIRM: Anton Kimball Design    DESIGNER: Anton Kimball    LETTERER: Anton Kimball and Bill Cameron    HEADLINE TYPEFACE: Custom    CLIENT: Misohapi Restaurant

29 DESIGN FIRM: Jager DiPaola Kemp Design    DESIGNER: Giovanna Jager    LETTERER: Giovanna Jager    CLIENT: Autumn Harp

30 DESIGN FIRM: GrandPre and Whaley, Ltd.    DESIGNER: Kevin Whaley    HEADLINE TYPEFACE: Univers    CLIENT: Chargo Printing, Inc.

31 DESIGN FIRM: University of Michigan    DESIGNER: Aaron D. King    HEADLINE TYPEFACE: Bodoni    CLIENT: University of Michigan College of Engineering

# HEAL'S <sup>32</sup>

33

34

32 DESIGN FIRM: *Lewis Moberly* DESIGNER: *Mary Lewis* LETTERER: *Mary Lewis* HEADLINE TYPEFACE: *Handlettering* CLIENT: *Heal & Son*

33 DESIGN FIRM: *Bruce Hale Design Studio* DESIGNER: *Bruce Hale* LETTERER: *Bruce Hale* HEADLINE TYPEFACE: *Handlettering* CLIENT: *Eddie Bauer*

34 DESIGN FIRM: *Executive Arts, Inc.* DESIGNER: *Phil Hamlett* LETTERER: *Phil Hamlett* HEADLINE TYPEFACE: *Rocket Bold (Custom)* CLIENT: *Philip Bekker Photo*

35

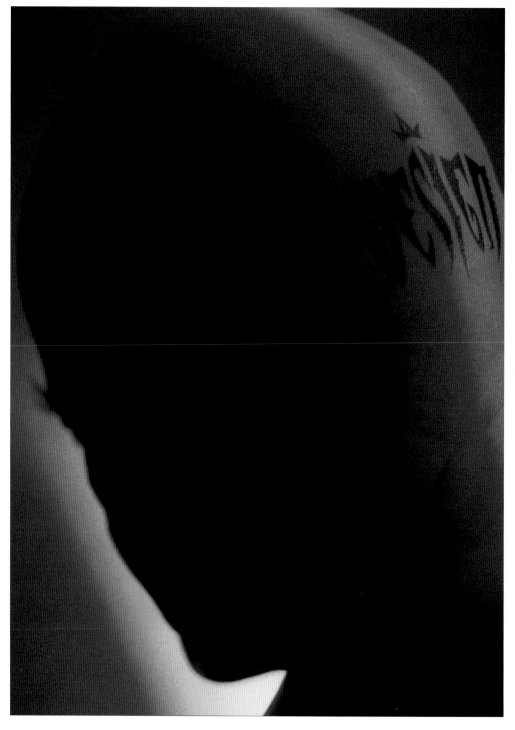

36

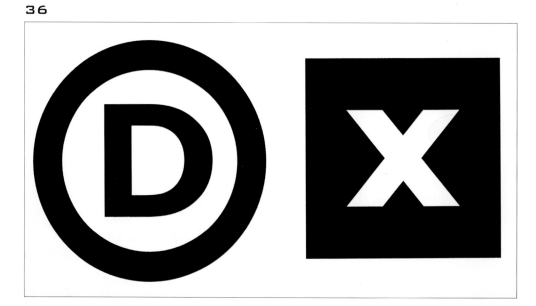

35 **DESIGN FIRM:** *Margo Chase Design*   **DESIGNER:** *Margo Chase*   **LETTERER:** *Margo Chase*   **CLIENT:** *Alternative Pick*

36 **DESIGN FIRM:** *Concrete Design Communications Inc.*   **DESIGNER:** *John Pylypczak and Diti Katona*   **HEADLINE TYPEFACE:** *Franklin Gothic*   **CLIENT:** *Design Exchange*

**37**

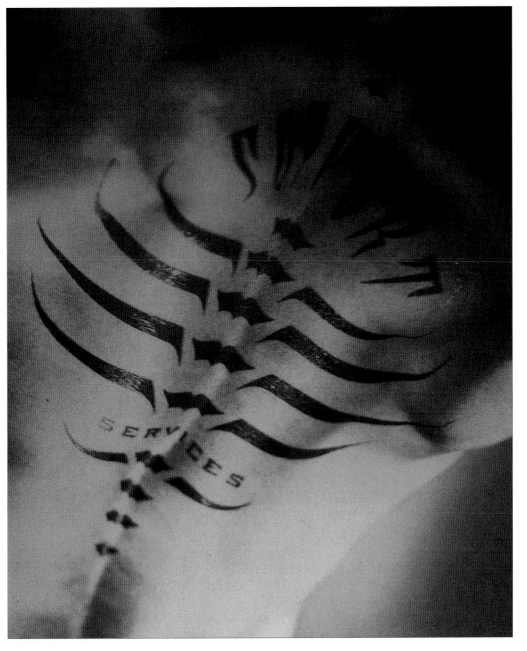

**38**

LOOMIS TRAIL

GOLF CLUB

37 **DESIGN FIRM:** *Margo Chase Design* **DESIGNER:** *Margo Chase* **LETTERER:** *Margo Chase* **CLIENT:** *Alternative Pick*

38 **DESIGN FIRM:** *The Leonhardt Group* **DESIGNER:** *Ray Ueno* **LETTERER:** *Ray Ueno* **HEADLINE TYPEFACE:** *New Baskerville* **CLIENT:** *Loomis Trail Golf Club*

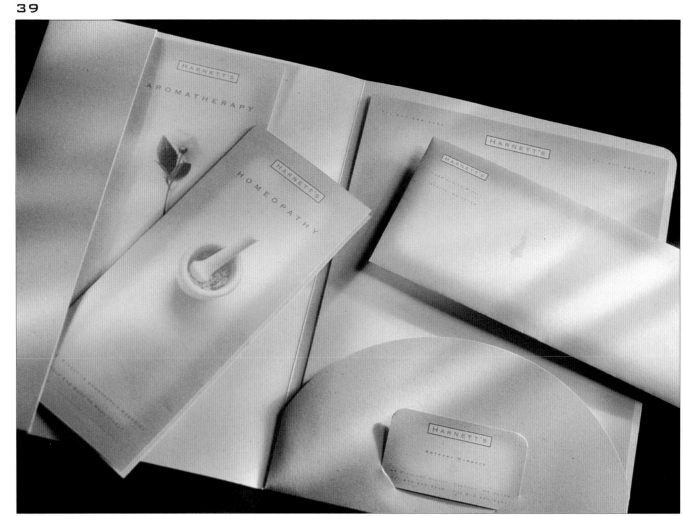

39  DESIGN FIRM: *Clifford Selbert Design*    DESIGNER: *Melanie Lowe*    LETTERER: *Melanie Lowe*    HEADLINE TYPEFACE: *Copperplate*    TEXT TYPEFACE: *Copperplate*    CLIENT: *Harnett's*

40  DESIGN FIRM: *Pinkhaus Design Corp.*    DESIGNER: *Tom Sterling and Mark Cantor*    LETTERER: *Tom Sterling*    TEXT TYPEFACE: *Industria*    CLIENT: *Pinkhaus Design Corp.*

41  DESIGN FIRM: *I.F. Planning Inc.*    DESIGNER: *Yukichi Takada*    LETTERER: *Yukichi Takada*    HEADLINE TYPEFACE: *Handlettering*    TEXT TYPEFACE: *Helvetica*    CLIENT: *I.F. Planning Inc.*

42 DESIGN FIRM: *Evenson Design Group* DESIGNER: *Glenn Sakamoto* HEADLINE TYPEFACE: *Bronzo (Modified)* TEXT TYPEFACE: *Bronzo* CLIENT: *Streamline Graphics*

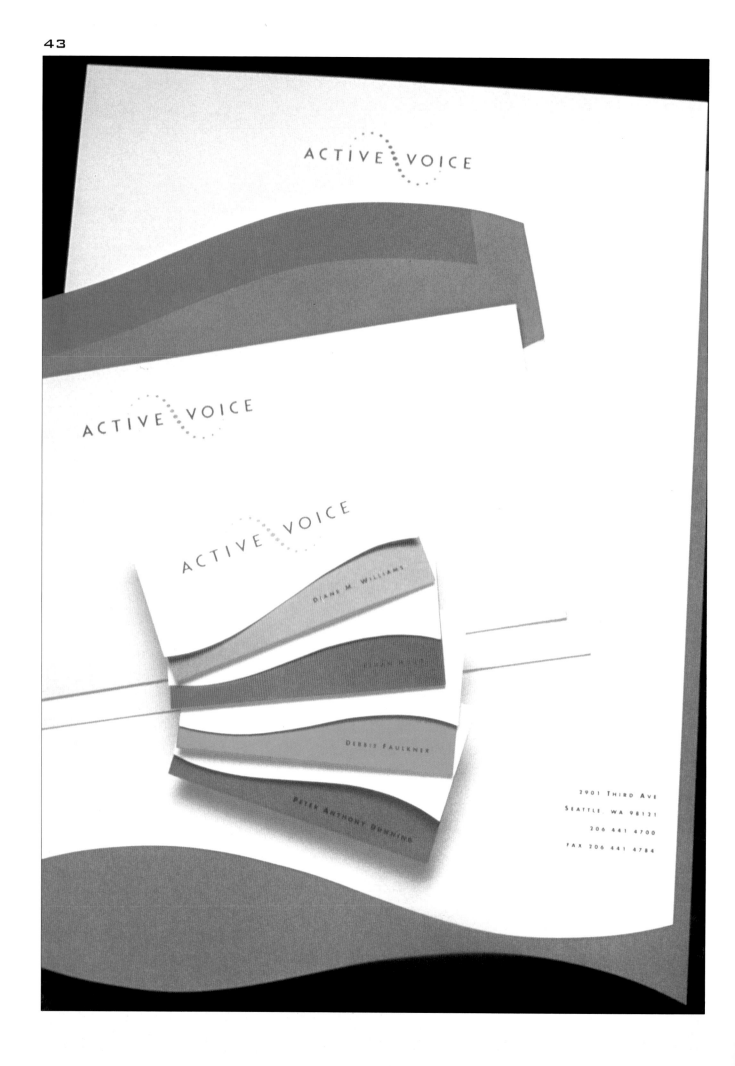

43  DESIGN FIRM: *Hornall Anderson Design Works*   DESIGNER: *Jack Anderson, Julia LaPine, David Bates, Mary Hermes and Lian Ng*   HEADLINE TYPEFACE: *Futura*   CLIENT: *Active Voice*

44  DESIGN FIRM: *Summerford Design, Inc.*   DESIGNER: *Jack Summerford*   HEADLINE TYPEFACE: *Various*   TEXT TYPEFACE: *Various*   CLIENT: *Summerford Design, Inc.*

45  DESIGN FIRM: *Sayles Graphic Design*   DESIGNER: *John Sayles*   LETTERER: *John Sayles*   HEADLINE TYPEFACE: *Brush Script*   TEXT TYPEFACE: *Typewritten and Hiroshige*   CLIENT: *Annie Meacham Creative*

46

47

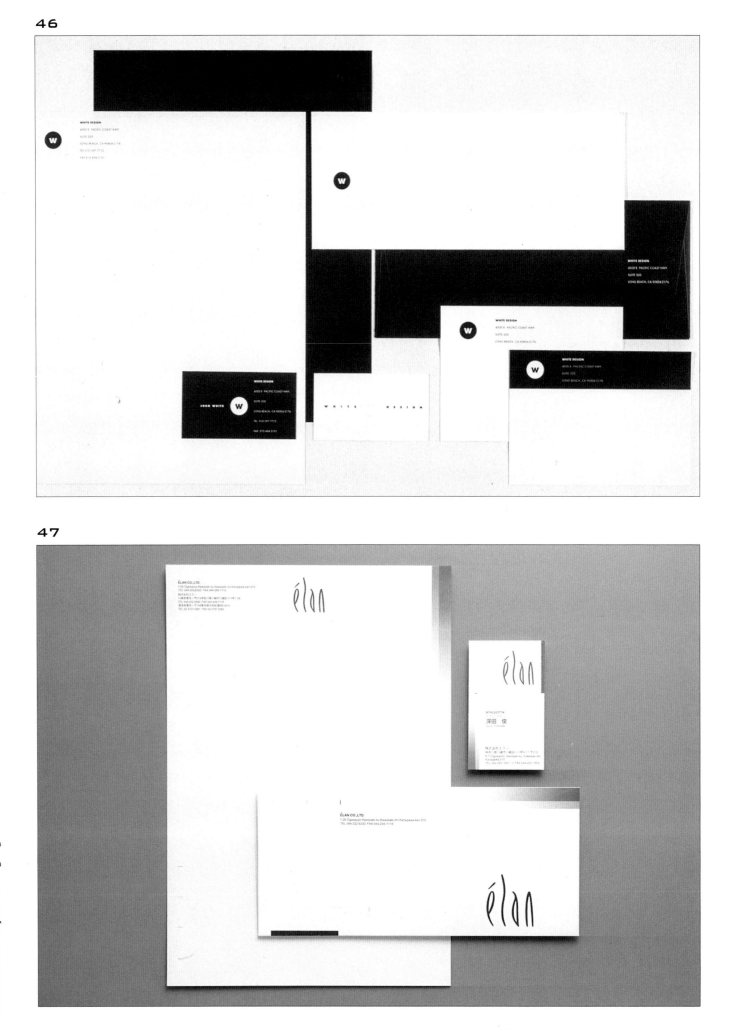

46  DESIGN FIRM: *White Design*  DESIGNER: *John White and Aram Youssefian*  HEADLINE TYPEFACE: *Futura Extrabold*  TEXT TYPEFACE: *Futura Book*  CLIENT: *White Design*

47  DESIGN FIRM: *Graphics & Designing Inc.*  DESIGNER: *Toshihiro Onimaru*  LETTERER: *Toshihiro Onimaru*  CLIENT: *Elan Co., Ltd.*

48 DESIGN FIRM: *After Hours*    DESIGNER: *Dino Paul*    HEADLINE TYPEFACE: *Futura Bold*    TEXT TYPEFACE: *Futura Bold*    CLIENT: *After Hours*

49 **DESIGN FIRM:** *Musser Design* **DESIGNER:** *Jerry Musser* **HEADLINE TYPEFACE:** *Univers 49* **TEXT TYPEFACE:** *Univers 49* **CLIENT:** *Extroverts*

50 **DESIGN FIRM:** *GrandPre and Whaley, Ltd.* **DESIGNER:** *Kevin Whaley* **HEADLINE TYPEFACE:** *Univers* **TEXT TYPEFACE:** *Univers* **CLIENT:** *Chargo Printing*

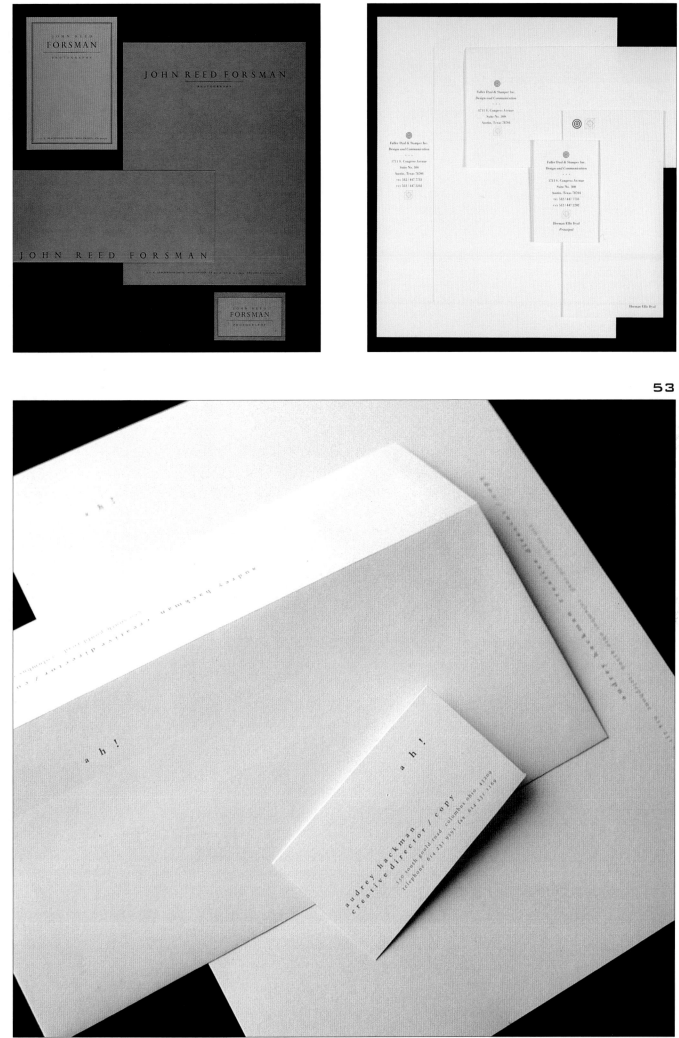

51  **DESIGN FIRM:** *Ph.D*  **DESIGNER:** *Michael Hodgson*  **HEADLINE TYPEFACE:** *Perpetua*  **TEXT TYPEFACE:** *Perpetua*  **CLIENT:** *John Reed Forsman*

52  **DESIGN FIRM:** *Fuller Dyal & Stamper*  **DESIGNER:** *Herman Dyal*  **TEXT TYPEFACE:** *Garamond*  **CLIENT:** *Fuller Dyal & Stamper*

53  **DESIGN FIRM:** *Schmeltz + Warren*  **DESIGNER:** *Crit Warren*  **TEXT TYPEFACE:** *Bembo*  **CLIENT:** *Audrey Hackman*

**55**

**56**

54 **DESIGN FIRM:** Segura Inc.  **DESIGNER:** Carlos Segura  **HEADLINE TYPEFACE:** Handlettering  **LETTERER:** Carlos Segura  **TEXT TYPEFACE:** Exocet  **CLIENT:** Segura Inc.

55 **DESIGN FIRM:** Vincent Lisi  **DESIGNER:** Vincent Lisi  **CLIENT:** Vincent Lisi  **LETTERER:** Vincent Lisi

56 **DESIGN FIRM:** Graphics & Designing Inc.  **DESIGNER:** Toshihiro Onimaru  **HEADLINE TYPEFACE:** Helvetica  **TEXT TYPEFACE:** Helvetica  **LETTERER:** Toshihiro Onimaru  **CLIENT:** Unix Corporation

57   DESIGN FIRM: *Hornall Anderson Design Works*    DESIGNER: *Julia LaPine and Denise Weir*    CLIENT: *Eagle Lake*

**44**

**58**

**59**

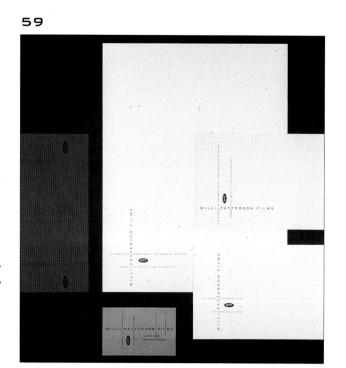

**60**

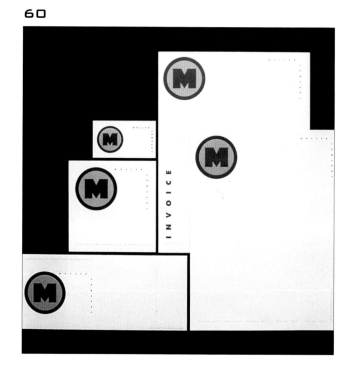

58 **DESIGN FIRM:** *The Leonhardt Group* **DESIGNER:** *Ray Ueno* **HEADLINE TYPEFACE:** *Franklin Gothic Heavy* **TEXT TYPEFACE:** *Franklin Gothic Heavy* **CLIENT:** *The Leonhardt Group*

59 **DESIGN FIRM:** *Ph.D* **DESIGNER:** *Michael Hodgson* **HEADLINE TYPEFACE:** *Copperplate* **TEXT TYPEFACE:** *Copperplate* **CLIENT:** *Willi Patterson Films*

60 **DESIGN FIRM:** *Muller + Company* **DESIGNER:** *John Muller* **HEADLINE TYPEFACE:** *Futura* **CLIENT:** *Muller + Company*

61

62

61  **DESIGN FIRM:** *Maureen Erbe Design*  **DESIGNER:** *Maureen Erbe and Rita Sowins*  **LETTERER:** *Maureen Erbe*  **HEADLINE TYPEFACE:** *Garamond 3 and Raleigh Gothic*  **TEXT TYPEFACE:** *Futura and Triplex*
    **CLIENT:** *Triumph*

62  **DESIGN FIRM:** *Tussel Lambie-Nairn*  **DESIGNER:** *Glenn Tussel*  **LETTERER:** *Tim Grey*  **HEADLINE TYPEFACE:** *Helvetica Bold*  **TEXT TYPEFACE:** *Helvetica Light*  **CLIENT:** *Wire TV*

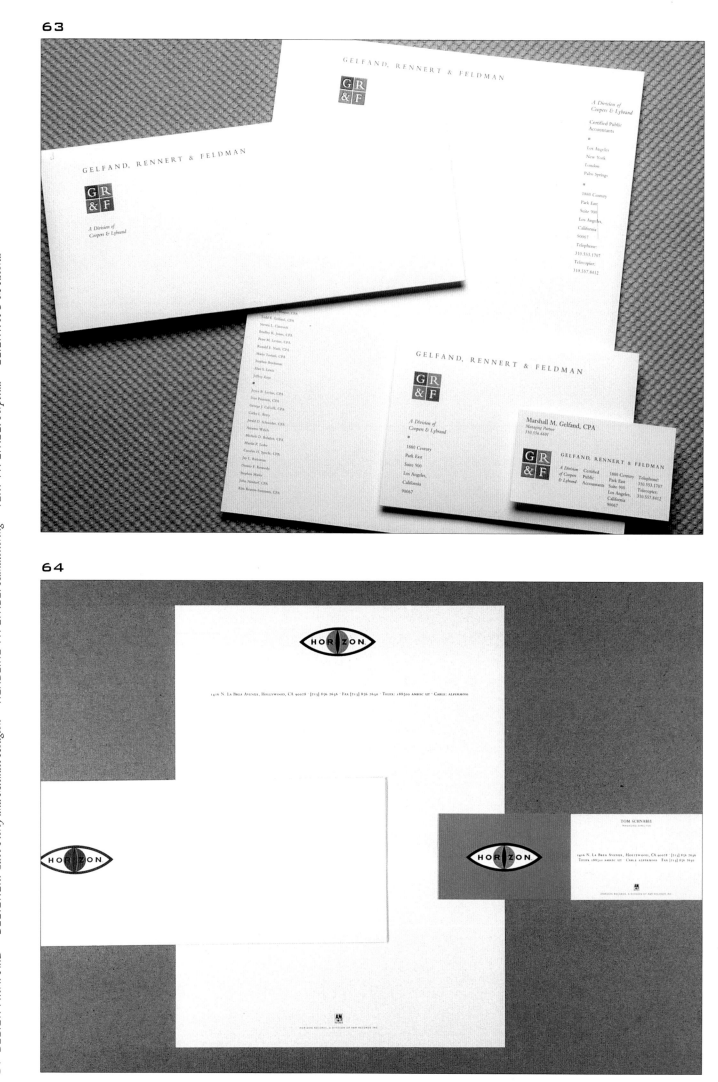

63  DESIGN FIRM: *Evenson Design Group*  DESIGNER: *Tricia Rauen*  HEADLINE TYPEFACE: *Bembo Semibold*  TEXT TYPEFACE: *Bembo Semibold*  CLIENT: *Gelfand, Rennert & Feldman*

64  DESIGN FIRM: *Ph.D*  DESIGNER: *Clive Piercy and Michael Hodgson*  HEADLINE TYPEFACE: *Handlettering*  TEXT TYPEFACE: *Perpetua*  CLIENT: *A & M Records*

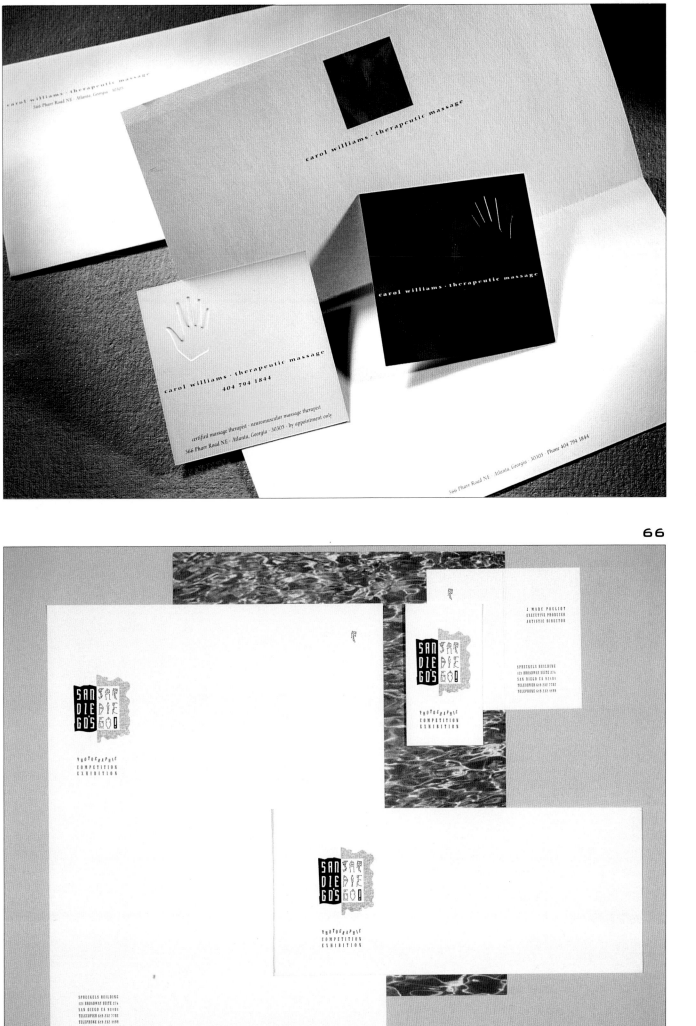

65 **DESIGN FIRM:** *Executive Arts, Inc.* **DESIGNER:** *Phil Hamlett* **HEADLINE TYPEFACE:** *Nofret* **TEXT TYPEFACE:** *Nofret* **CLIENT:** *Carol Williams*

66 **DESIGN FIRM:** *Visual Asylum* **DESIGNER:** *Mae Lin Levine and David Jervis* **HEADLINE TYPEFACE:** *Handlettering* **HEADLINE TYPEFACE:** *Sempel Shadow Black Condensed* **CLIENT:** *j marc Pouliot/Berkmar Group*

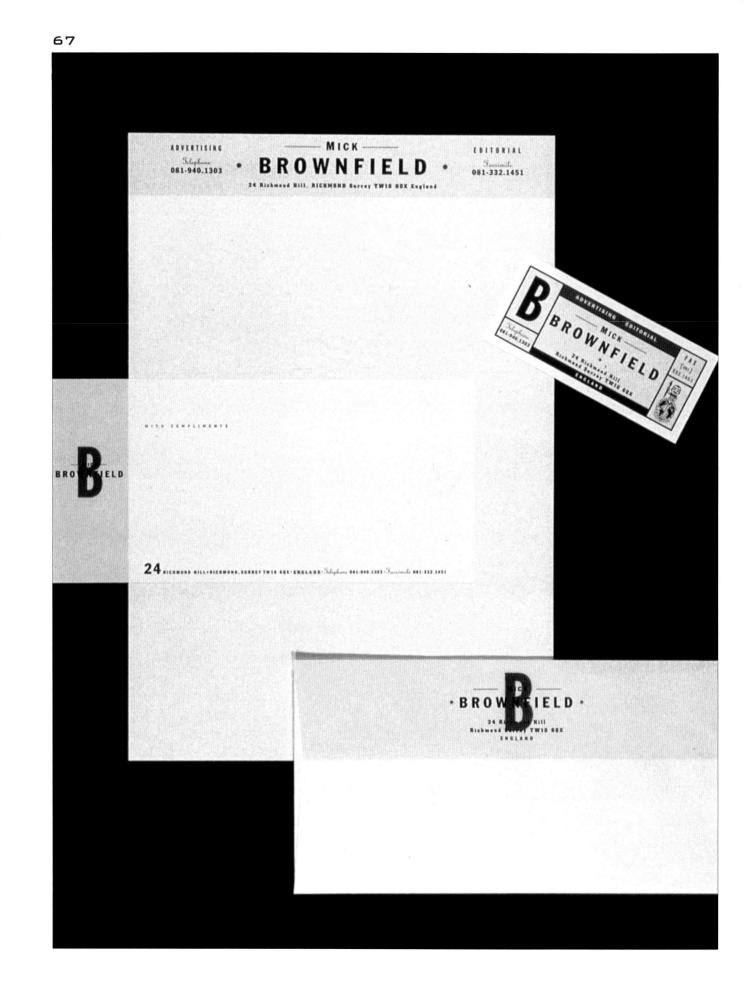

67 DESIGN FIRM: *Ph.D* DESIGNER: *Clive Piercy* HEADLINE TYPEFACE: *Franklin Gothic* TEXT TYPEFACE: *Franklin and Linoscript* CLIENT: *Mick Brownfield*

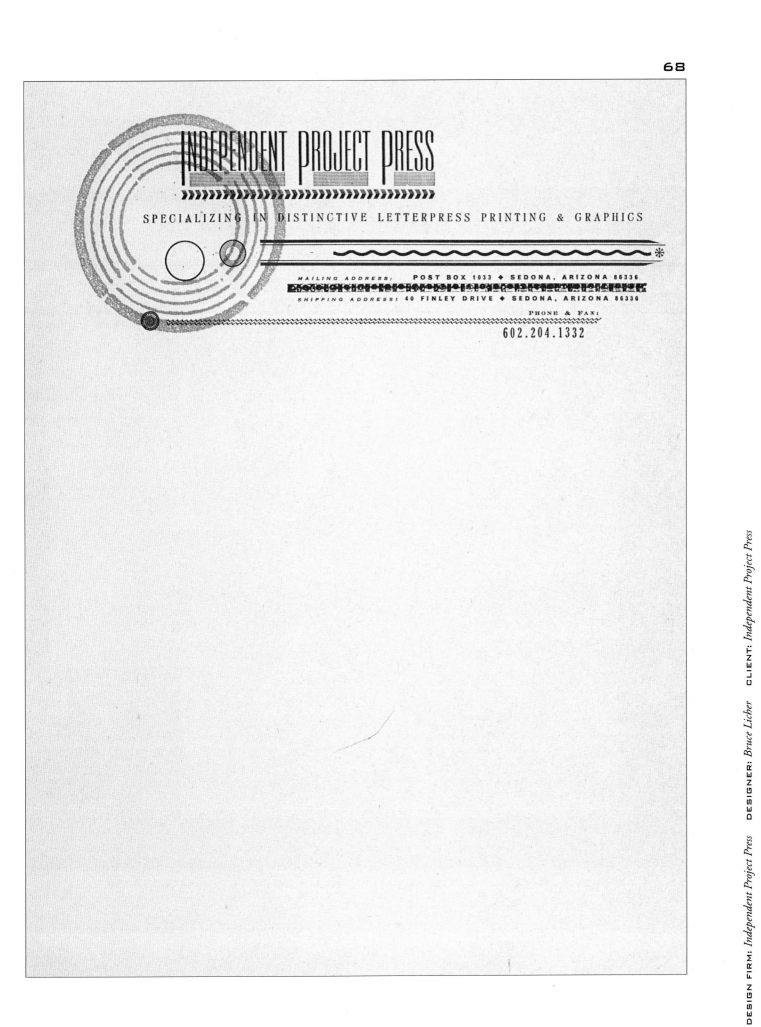

# INDEPENDENT PROJECT PRESS

SPECIALIZING IN DISTINCTIVE LETTERPRESS PRINTING & GRAPHICS

MAILING ADDRESS: POST BOX 1033 ◆ SEDONA, ARIZONA 86336

SHIPPING ADDRESS: 40 FINLEY DRIVE ◆ SEDONA, ARIZONA 86336

PHONE & FAX:

602.204.1332

68 DESIGN FIRM: *Independent Project Press*   DESIGNER: *Bruce Licher*   CLIENT: *Independent Project Press*

DESIGN FIRM: *Lorna Stovall Design*   DESIGNER: *Lorna Stovall*   HEADLINE TYPEFACE: *Stadion*   TEXT TYPEFACE: *Bank Gothic*   CLIENT: *Machine Head*

69

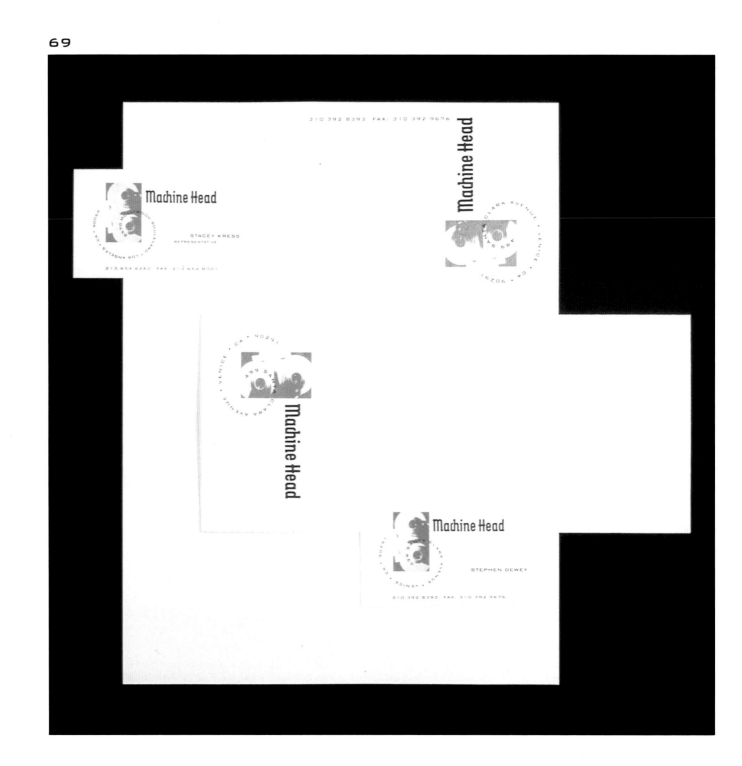

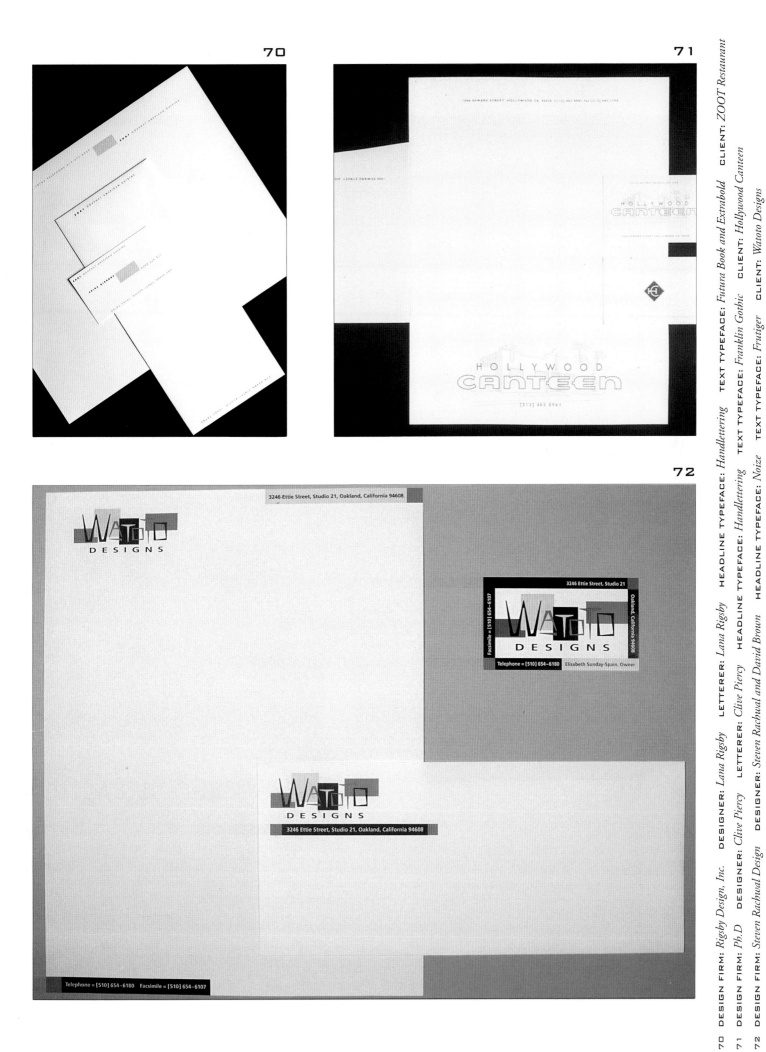

**70**    DESIGN FIRM: *Rigsby Design, Inc.*    DESIGNER: *Lana Rigsby*    LETTERER: *Lana Rigsby*    HEADLINE TYPEFACE: *Handlettering*    TEXT TYPEFACE: *Futura Book and Extrabold*    CLIENT: *ZOOT Restaurant*

**71**    DESIGN FIRM: *Ph.D*    DESIGNER: *Clive Piercy*    LETTERER: *Clive Piercy*    HEADLINE TYPEFACE: *Handlettering*    TEXT TYPEFACE: *Franklin Gothic*    CLIENT: *Hollywood Canteen*

**72**    DESIGN FIRM: *Steven Rachwal Design*    DESIGNER: *Steven Rachwal and David Brown*    HEADLINE TYPEFACE: *Noize*    TEXT TYPEFACE: *Frutiger*    CLIENT: *Watoto Designs*

**73**

**74**

73 **DESIGN FIRM:** *Tor Pettersen & Partners Ltd.* **DESIGNER:** *Tor Pettersen, Paul Mann, Jeff Davis and Sarah Stevens-Jones* **CLIENT:** *Cable & Wireless PLC*

74 **DESIGN FIRM:** *Lippincott & Margulies* **DESIGNER:** *Dennis Favello* **TEXT TYPEFACE:** *Trade Gothic Regular Extended* **CLIENT:** *SONY Music Entertainment Inc.*

75  DESIGN FIRM: *Pentagram Design Ltd.*  DESIGNER: *David Pocknell*  LETTERER: *David Pocknell*  HEADLINE TYPEFACE: *New Johnston Medium*  TEXT TYPEFACE: *Bembo*  CLIENT: *London Transport*

PROMOTION

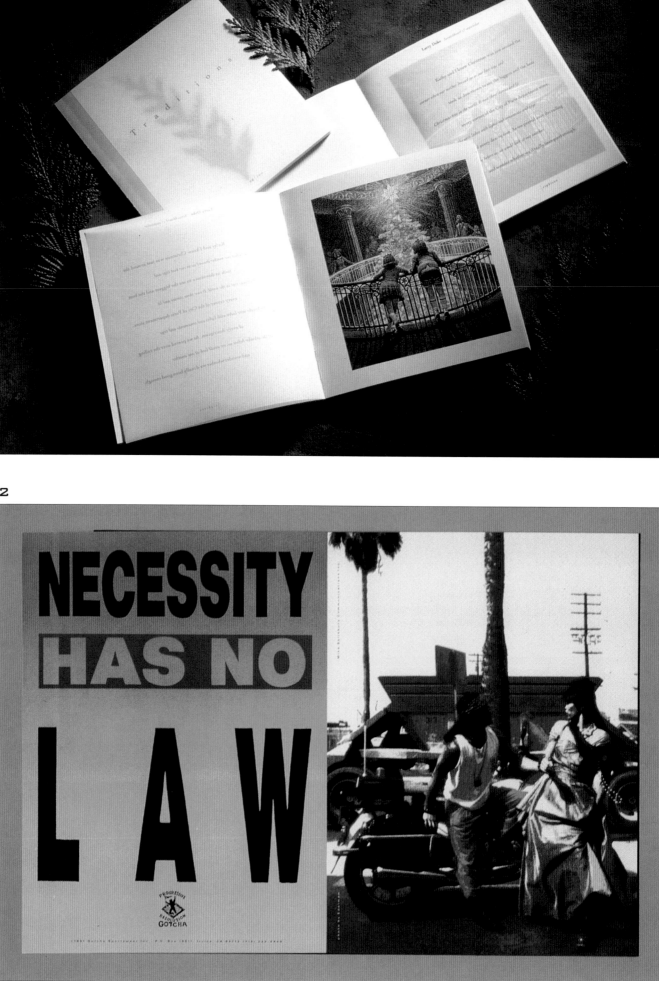

**1**

**2**

1  **DESIGN FIRM:** *The Leonhardt Group*  **DESIGNER:** *Traci Daberkow*  **HEADLINE TYPEFACE:** *Cochin*  **TEXT TYPEFACE:** *Cochin*  **CLIENT:** *Pat Hackett, Artist Rep.*

2  **DESIGN FIRM:** *Mike Salisbury Communications, Inc.*  **DESIGNER:** *Mike Salisbury*  **LETTERER:** *Mike Salisbury*  **HEADLINE TYPEFACE:** *Helvetica and Sausbury*  **CLIENT:** *Gotcha Sports Wear*

**3** **DESIGN FIRM:** *Vaughn Wedeen Creative* **DESIGNER:** *Dan Flynn* **HEADLINE TYPEFACE:** *Coronet, Mercurius Script, Futura Condensed and Franklin Gothic* **CLIENT:** *Vaughn Wedeen Creative*

58

4 DESIGN FIRM: Parham Santana Inc.    DESIGNER: Rick Stermole    HEADLINE TYPEFACE: Bodoni and Helvetica Black    TEXT TYPEFACE: Bodoni and Helvetica Bold    CLIENT: Kaplan

5 DESIGN FIRM: Parham Santana Inc.    DESIGNER: Rick Stermole    HEADLINE TYPEFACE: Swiss 921 and Helvetica Black    TEXT TYPEFACE: Bodoni, Kuenstler Script and Helvetica Bold    CLIENT: Kaplan

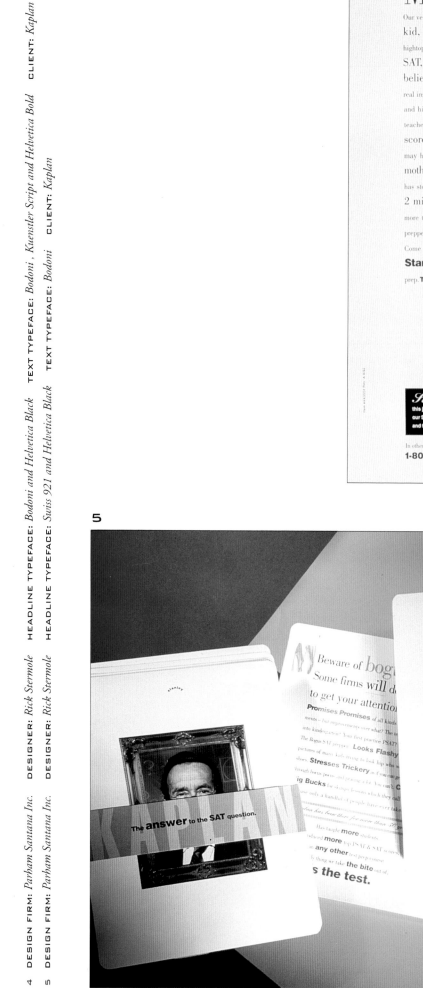

**6**

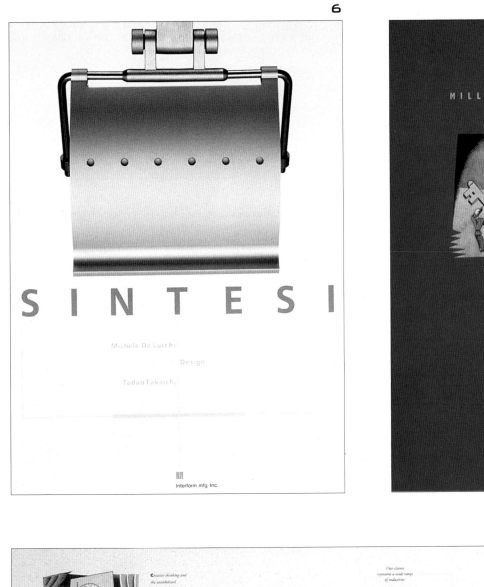

**7**

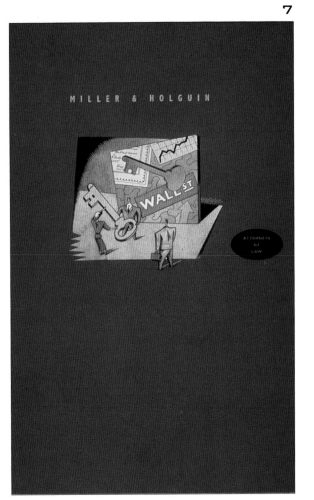

**8**

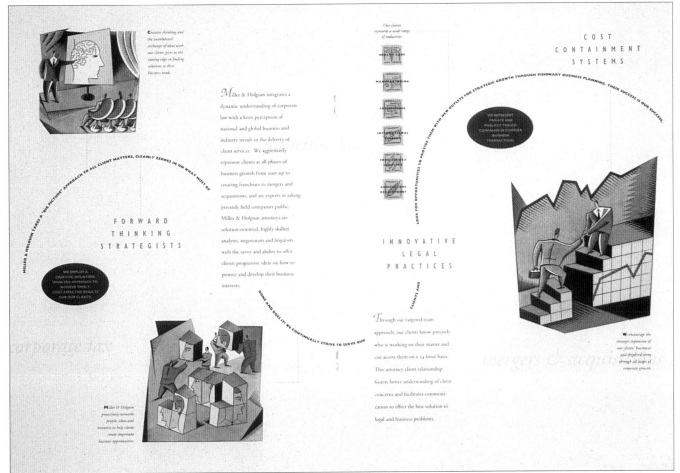

6  DESIGN FIRM: *Jun Sato Design Inc.*  DESIGNER: *Jun Sato*  LETTERER: *Jun Sato*  HEADLINE TYPEFACE: *Frutiger Bold*  TEXT TYPEFACE: *Univers Medium 55*  CLIENT: *Interform Mfg., Inc.*

7  DESIGN FIRM: *White Design*  DESIGNER: *Susan Garland Foti*  HEADLINE TYPEFACE: *Gill Sans Condensed*  TEXT TYPEFACE: *Adobe Garamond Regular*  CLIENT: *Miller and Holguin*

8  DESIGN FIRM: *White Design*  DESIGNER: *Susan Garland Foti*  HEADLINE TYPEFACE: *Gill Sans Condensed*  TEXT TYPEFACE: *Adobe Garamond Regular*  CLIENT: *Miller and Holguin*

**9**

**10**

**11**

9 DESIGN FIRM: *Concrete Design Communications, Inc.* DESIGNER: *Diti Katona and John Pylypczak* HEADLINE TYPEFACE: *Franklin Gothic* CLIENT: *Casey House*

10 DESIGN FIRM: *Concrete Design Communications, Inc.* DESIGNER: *Diti Katona and John Pylypczak* HEADLINE TYPEFACE: *Franklin Gothic* CLIENT: *Casey House*

11 DESIGN FIRM: *Musser Design* DESIGNER: *Jerry Musser* HEADLINE TYPEFACE: *Univers* TEXT TYPEFACE: *Univers* CLIENT: *Armstrong World Industries*

12 **DESIGN FIRM:** *Hornall Anderson Design Works*   **DESIGNER:** *Jack Anderson, Heidi Hatlestad, Bruce Branson-Meyer*   **HEADLINE TYPEFACE:** *Futura*   **TEXT TYPEFACE:** *Weiss*   **CLIENT:** *Six Sigma*

13 **DESIGN FIRM:** *Segura Inc.*   **DESIGNER:** *Carlos Segura*   **HEADLINE TYPEFACE:** *Carlos Segura*   **LETTERER:** *Carlos Segura*   **TEXT TYPEFACE:** *Centaur*   **HEADLINE TYPEFACE:** *Centaur*   **TEXT TYPEFACE:** *Centaur*   **CLIENT:** *John Cleland*

**14**

**15**

LOCATION!

LOCATION!

LOCATION!

IT'S NOT EASY MOVING CONCRETE

*Well – not having ever heeded conventional wisdom before, we're bucking the trend and moving west! So, as of May 4, 1992, you will find us in our new (and freshly painted!) offices at 2 Silver Avenue.*

**CONCRETE**

PHONE: 534-9960  FACSIMILE: 534-2184  MODEM: 534-9707

2 SILVER AVENUE, MAIN FLOOR, TORONTO, ONTARIO, M6R 3A2

**16**

14  **DESIGN FIRM:** *Graphiculture*  **DESIGNER:** *Cheryl Watson*  **TEXT TYPEFACE:** *Times Roman and Franklin Gothic*  **CLIENT:** *Graphiculture*

15  **DESIGN FIRM:** *Concrete Design Communications, Inc.*  **DESIGNER:** *Diti Katona and John Pylypczak*  **HEADLINE TYPEFACE:** *Centaur*  **TEXT TYPEFACE:** *Centaur*  **CLIENT:** *Concrete Design Communications, Inc.*

16  **DESIGN FIRM:** *Hornall Anderson Design Works*  **DESIGNER:** *Jack Anderson, Paula Cox and David Bates*  **TEXT TYPEFACE:** *Weiss*  **CLIENT:** *Hornall Anderson Design Works*

HEADLINE TYPEFACE: *Univers Extended Extra Black*   CLIENT: *Microsoft*

TEXT TYPEFACE: *Adobe Sabon*   CLIENT: *William Drenttel New York*

LETTERER: *Traci Daberkow*   DESIGNER: *Traci Daberkow*   HEADLINE TYPEFACE: *Adobe Sabon*   DESIGNER: *Stephen Doyle*

17   DESIGN FIRM: *The Leonhardt Group*

18   DESIGN FIRM: *Drenttel Doyle Partners*

**19**

**20**

**21**

19  DESIGN FIRM: *Zimmermann Crowe Design*   DESIGNER: *Neal Zimmerman and Dennis Crowe*   HEADLINE TYPEFACE: *Bank Gothic and Franklin Gothic*   CLIENT: *Zimmermann Crowe Design*

20  DESIGN FIRM: *Zimmermann Crowe Design*   DESIGNER: *Neal Zimmerman and Dennis Crowe*   HEADLINE TYPEFACE: *Matrix In-line/Bank Gothic*   TEXT TYPEFACE: *Garamond*   CLIENT: *Fong & Fong Printing*

21  DESIGN FIRM: *Concrete Design Communications, Inc.*   DESIGNER: *Diti Katona*   LETTERER: *John Pylypczak*   CLIENT: *Zapata*

23 **DESIGN FIRM:** *Vrontikis Design Office* **DESIGNER:** *Petrula Vrontikis* **HEADLINE TYPEFACE:** *Sharp Fax Machine* **TEXT TYPEFACE:** *Sharp Fax Machine* **CLIENT:** *E! Entertainment Television*

24 **DESIGN FIRM:** *Peterson & Company* **DESIGNER:** *Scott Paramski* **LETTERER:** *Mary Lynn Blasutta* **HEADLINE TYPEFACE:** *Gill Sans* **TEXT TYPEFACE:** *Times* **CLIENT:** *Federal Reserves*

In determining monetary policy, the Federal Reserve must consider what is best for the nation's economy as a whole. When events such as energy price shocks occur, these decisions are much more difficult because of short-term inflationary and recessionary pressures on the economy. Over the long term, however, the Fed's monetary policy actions are based on an overriding objective of fostering steady growth in all segments of the economy.

**25**

INDEPENDENT PRO JECT PRESS

**!**

TYPEFACES
AND
ORNAMENTS

SECOND EDITION

544 MATEO STREET
LOS ANGELES ◉ CALIF. 90013

PHONE & FAX:
213.617.3294

**26**

THE INDEPENDENT PROJECT SHOP

1307 PALMETTO STREET
AT MATEO STREET
IN DOWNTOWN LOS ANGELES

telefon 213 ◆ 617 ◆ 3294

TEXT TYPEFACE: *Futura Bold and Bodoni* CLIENT: *Univ. of Cal., Santa Barbara*

HEADLINE TYPEFACE: *Handlettering* TEXT TYPEFACE: *Handlettering*

LETTERER: *John Sayles* CLIENT: *The Independent Project Shop* CLIENT: *Independent Project Press*

DESIGNER: *John Sayles* DESIGNER: *Bruce Licher* DESIGNER: *Bruce Licher*

25 DESIGN FIRM: *Independent Project Press*
26 DESIGN FIRM: *Independent Project Press*
27 DESIGN FIRM: *Sayles Graphic Design*

**28**

**29**

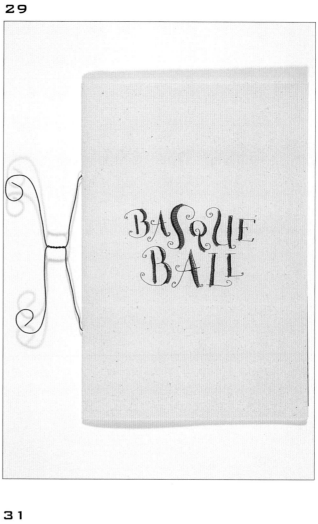

**30**

IMPRESSIONS

**31**

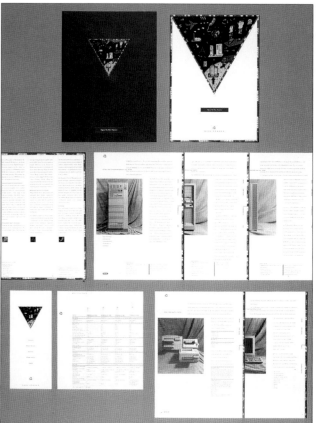

28  DESIGN FIRM: After Hours    DESIGNER: Todd Ferell    HEADLINE TYPEFACE: Journal    TEXT TYPEFACE: Journal    CLIENT: Casa de San Pedro

29  DESIGN FIRM: Fuller Dyal & Stamper    DESIGNER: Herman Dyal    LETTERER: Herman Dyal    HEADLINE TYPEFACE: Handlettering    TEXT TYPEFACE: Garamond    CLIENT: Contemporary Arts Museum

30  DESIGN FIRM: Fiorentino Associates    DESIGNER: Helen Fiorentino    HEADLINE TYPEFACE: Garamond    TEXT TYPEFACE: Garamond with Italics    CLIENT: KBA-Planeta North America, Inc.

31  DESIGN FIRM: Cipriani Kremer Design    DESIGNER: Toni Bowerman    HEADLINE TYPEFACE: Bauer Bodoni and Helvetica    TEXT TYPEFACE: Bauer Bodoni and Helvetica    CLIENT: Wang

32  **DESIGN FIRM:** *Maureen Erbe Design*  **DESIGNER:** *Maureen Erbe and Rita Sowins*  **HEADLINE TYPEFACE:** *Bernhard Modern Roman*  **TEXT TYPEFACE:** *Futura*  **CLIENT:** *California Institute of Technology*

**LETTERER:** *Julia Daggett*  **HEADLINE TYPEFACE:** *Liberty and Bernhard Modern*

33  **DESIGN FIRM:** *Clifford Selbert Design, Inc.*  **DESIGNER:** *Julia Daggett, Bob Merk and Heather Watson*  **CLIENT:** *Boston Design Center*

**TEXT TYPEFACE:** *Bernhard Modern*

34  **DESIGN FIRM:** *Evenson Design Group*   **DESIGNER:** *Stan Evenson*   **HEADLINE TYPEFACE:** *Caslon 540*   **TEXT TYPEFACE:** *Caslon 540*   **CLIENT:** *Evenson Design Group*

35  **DESIGN FIRM:** *The Leonhardt Group*   **DESIGNER:** *Traci Daberkow and Janet Kruse*   **HEADLINE TYPEFACE:** *Nuptial Script*   **TEXT TYPEFACE:** *Cochin*   **CLIENT:** *Pacific Northwest Wine Coalition*

## 36

We stimulate aspiring artists to confront their individual creative powers. For our world of intense competition and rapid change, we prepare individuals with confidence, self-reliance, integrity, and responsibility. Julian Stanczak

# pAiNtiNg

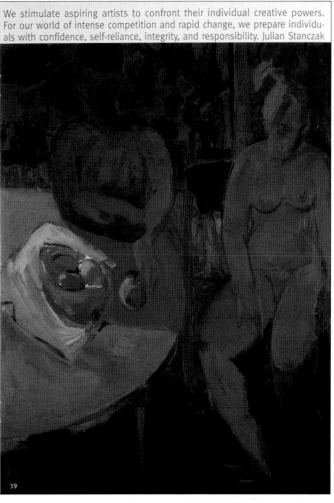

By teaching both perceptual and conceptual approaches, we aim for a comprehensive understanding of painting — one that is intellectual, physical, and intuitive. Kenneth Dingwall

**Painting.** Painting students learn the theory and practice of painting from a widely experienced faculty of committed painters whose works have been exhibited and collected throughout the US and abroad. Painting students also learn from one another. Their individual studios are well designed for them to observe the growth of each other's work, to exchange attitudes, and to learn how to respond to diverse ideas and forms through one-on-one teaching and group critiques. We encourage students to define and express their own ideas, rather than be limited by any dogma or trend.     CIA's proximity to a world-class art museum and a large contemporary art center allows students to continually update their knowledge of the history and current climate of painting. It also challenges their aesthetic sense and generates a feeling of belonging to an ancient and ongoing community of painters. Other catalysts for students' growth are visits by distinguished artists and a new program to exchange painting students with British art schools.     Our thorough attention to each student leads to the self-discipline and depth of perception that are needed in pragmatic fields. Painting graduates have succeeded in graduate school, teaching, art administration, operation of galleries and museums, and as practicing, exhibiting artists.

38
39

some things satisfy in a way we intuitively know is best.

36  DESIGN FIRM: *Nesnadny + Schwartz*   DESIGNER: *Joyce Nesnadny and Brian Lavy*   HEADLINE TYPEFACE: *Bodoni*   TEXT TYPEFACE: *Meta*   CLIENT: *Cleveland Institute of Art*

37  DESIGN FIRM: *Ph.D*   DESIGNER: *Clive Piercy and Michael Hodgson*   HEADLINE TYPEFACE: *Gill Sans*   TEXT TYPEFACE: *Gill Sans and Sabon*   CLIENT: *American Seating*

**38**

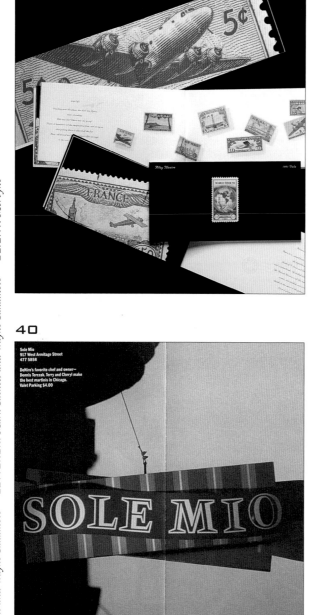

**39**

retire
ment
or...
made easy™

**40**

Sole Mio
917 West Armitage Street
477 5858

DeNiro's favorite chef and owner—
Dennis Terczak, Terry and Cheryl make
the best martinis in Chicago.
Valet Parking $4.00

SOLE MIO

**41**

An informal look at some of the things that go into, and come out of, annual reports.

Although every public corporation publishes a report every
year, it has never been easy to get it right—the right look, the
right feel, the right tone, the right balance of the right mix.

The right Neenah paper is part of it (just as it is in so many other significant print products). That's why once
again we are sending you a portfolio of observations about, and views of, what goes on in annual reports—
their styles, their themes, their uses.          This has been a very good year for Neenah Paper. In
annual report terms, our product consistency, professional standards, and inventory levels
have remained outstanding,          while our line has expanded to reflect our
closeness to customers' needs. At Neenah Paper, standing for the highest quality has
not meant standing still.

**Neenah Paper**
Oil and Water

**42**

38  DESIGN FIRM: *Rigsby Design, Inc.*    DESIGNER: *Lana Rigsby*    HEADLINE TYPEFACE: *Nuptial Script*    TEXT TYPEFACE: *Futura Condensed and Nuptial Script*    CLIENT: *The Alley Theatre*

39  DESIGN FIRM: *Carol Piechocki*    DESIGNER: *Carol Piechocki*    HEADLINE TYPEFACE: *Univers 67*    TEXT TYPEFACE: *Bodoni Book*    CLIENT: *Aetna*

40  DESIGN FIRM: *Kym Abrams Design/Sam Silvio Design*    DESIGNER: *Kym Abrams/Sam Silvio*    TEXT TYPEFACE: *Franklin Gothic Condensed*    CLIENT: *American Institute of Design/Chicago*

41  DESIGN FIRM: *Grady, Campbell, Inc.*    DESIGNER: *Kerry Grady*    LETTERER: *Kerry Grady*    HEADLINE TYPEFACE: *Univers*    TEXT TYPEFACE: *Univers*    CLIENT: *Neenah Paper*

42  DESIGN FIRM: *Sackett Design*    DESIGNER: *Mark Sackett and Wayne Sakamoto*    LETTERER: *Mark Sackett and Wayne Sakamoto*    CLIENT: *Mervyn's*

**44**

**45**

44 **DESIGN FIRM:** *Lisa Levin Design* **DESIGNER:** *Lisa Levin* **HEADLINE TYPEFACE:** *Futura* **TEXT TYPEFACE:** *Copperplate and Garamond* **CLIENT:** *Specialized Bicycles*

45 **DESIGN FIRM:** *Vaughn Wedeen Creative* **DESIGNER:** *Rick Vaughn* **HEADLINE TYPEFACE:** *Various* **TEXT TYPEFACE:** *Various* **CLIENT:** *QC Graphics*

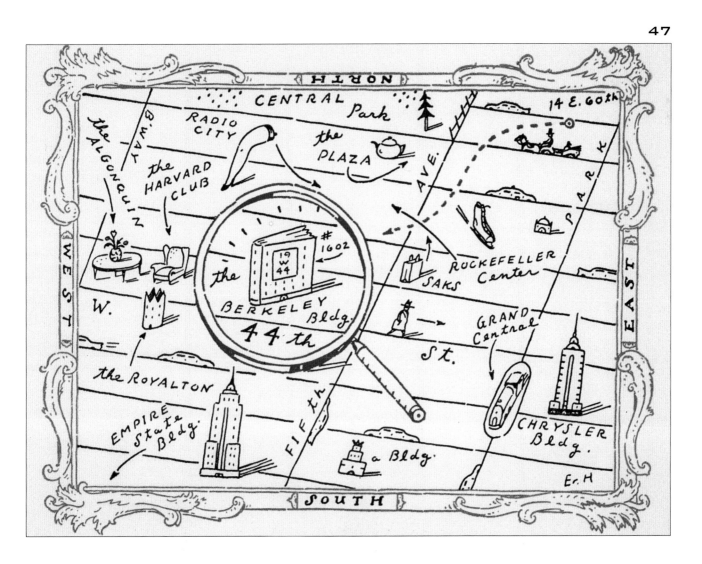

46 DESIGN FIRM: DBD International, Ltd.   DESIGNER: David Brier   HEADLINE TYPEFACE: Various   TEXT TYPEFACE: Various   CLIENT: DBD International, Ltd.

47 DESIGN FIRM: Robert Valentine Incorporated   DESIGNER: Robert Valentine   LETTERER: David Brier   HEADLINE TYPEFACE: Sabon and M Garamond   TEXT TYPEFACE: Sabon and M Garamond   CLIENT: Authors and Artists Group

48

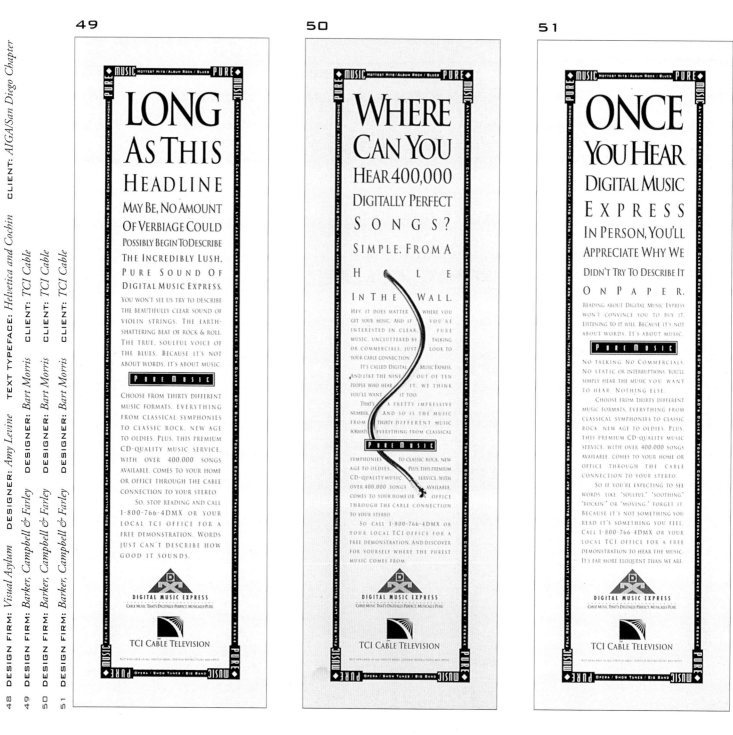

48 DESIGN FIRM: *Visual Asylum* DESIGNER: *Amy Levine* TEXT TYPEFACE: *Helvetica and Cochin* CLIENT: *AIGA/San Diego Chapter*

49 DESIGN FIRM: *Barker, Campbell & Farley* DESIGNER: *Bart Morris* CLIENT: *TCI Cable*

50 DESIGN FIRM: *Barker, Campbell & Farley* DESIGNER: *Bart Morris* CLIENT: *TCI Cable*

51 DESIGN FIRM: *Barker, Campbell & Farley* DESIGNER: *Bart Morris* CLIENT: *TCI Cable*

52

The Big Idea Behind The Big Ideas. We even take an integrated approach to strategic thinking. Which means our marketing people work with o[...]p marketing solutions that [...] strategy. And it's ideas like [...]place. The work on these [...] striking example of the

What is a marketing agency, anyway? Good question. Unfortunately, the answer you receive depends on who you ask. And the reason is simple. As the marketplace becomes more competitive, corporations like yours are discovering that advertising is just not enough. [...]

You always need more. You need to drive sales. And you need creative solutions that cut across a wide spectrum of disciplines. So in an attempt to fill this void, everyone is suddenly telling you they can do it all. But former direct marketing agencies that are now "integrated agencies" will suspiciously provide you with solutions that are primarily [...] direct mail executions. And former sales promotion agencies now calling themselves marketing agencies will come up with sales promotion ideas.

At U.S. Communications, being a marketing agency is not just some handy label to attract new business. It's who we are.

SBSS II
SYSTEM 7 COMPATIBLE

MS·DOS Disk

SBSS II

Small Business Sa[...]

Using integrated business solutions to build customers, sales and profit.

53

KROMEKOTE

ONE · SUBJECTIVE REASONING

THE END

OF COMMUNISM
IS A MESSAGE TO THE
HUMAN RACE.

EXCERPTED FROM A SPEECH BY
VACLAV HAVEL
PRESIDENT OF THE CZECH AND SLOVAK FEDERAL REPUBLIC
AT THE WORLD ECONOMIC FORUM
FEBRUARY 4, 1992

52 DESIGN FIRM: Rapp Collins Communications DESIGNER: Jo Davidson Strand CLIENT: Rapp Collins Communications DESIGNER: Jo Davidson Strand CLIENT: Champion International TEXT TYPEFACE: Hand-rendered Bembo HEADLINE TYPEFACE: Hand-rendered Bembo

53 DESIGN FIRM: Drenttel Doyle Partners/Pentagram DESIGNER: Stephen Doyle

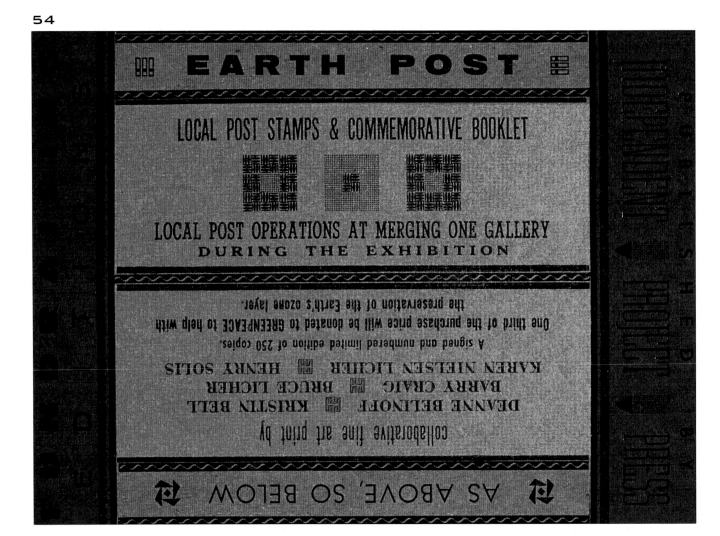

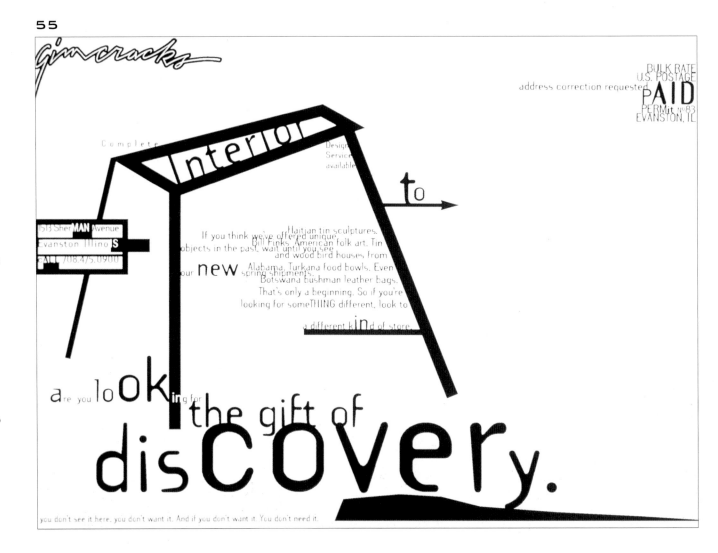

54 **DESIGN FIRM:** Independent Project Press  **DESIGNER:** Bruce Licher  **CLIENT:** Independent Project Press

55 **DESIGN FIRM:** Segura Inc.  **DESIGNER:** Carlos Segura  **CLIENT:** Gimcracks

Adrian Piper. WHAT IT'S LIKE, WHAT IT IS, #3. 1991. Photo © Scott Frances/Esto

DISLOC
ATIONS

THE MUSEUM OF MODERN ART, NEW YORK

56  DESIGN FIRM: *Samata Associates*   DESIGNER: *Pat and Greg Samata*   HEADLINE TYPEFACE: *Lithos Black*   TEXT TYPEFACE: *Lithos Regular*   CLIENT: *Appleton Papers, Inc.*

57  DESIGN FIRM: *Samata Associates*   DESIGNER: *Pat and Greg Samata*   HEADLINE TYPEFACE: *Lithos Black*   TEXT TYPEFACE: *Lithos Regular*   CLIENT: *Appleton Papers, Inc.*

58  DESIGN FIRM: *Drenttel Doyle Partners*   DESIGNER: *Andy Grey*   HEADLINE TYPEFACE: *Monotype Centaur*   TEXT TYPEFACE: *Monotype Centaur*   CLIENT: *Museum of Modern Art*

**59**

**60**

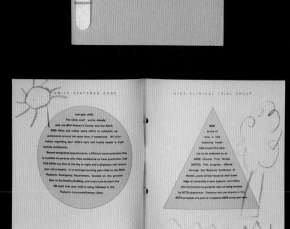

**61**

**62**

**63**

59 DESIGN FIRM: *Parham Santana Inc.* DESIGNER: *Okey Nestor* HEADLINE TYPEFACE: *Industria* TEXT TYPEFACE: *Matrix, Industria and Helvetica Black* CLIENT: *VH-1 Marketing Comm./MTV Networks*

60 DESIGN FIRM: *Runnion Design* DESIGNER: *Jeff and Allie Runnion* HEADLINE TYPEFACE: *Eurostyle Regular* TEXT TYPEFACE: *Eurostyle Bold* CLIENT: *Boston City Hospital*

61 DESIGN FIRM: *Stewart Monderer Design, Inc.* DESIGNER: *Robert S. Davidson/Jane Winsor* LETTERER: *Mark Matcho* HEADLINE TYPEFACE: *Linoscript (altered)* TEXT TYPEFACE: *Garamond #3* CLIENT: *Fox River Paper Company*

*Stewart Monderer Design, Inc.*

62 DESIGN FIRM: *Van Dyke Company* DESIGNER: *John Van Dyke and Ann Kumasaka* HEADLINE TYPEFACE: *Various* TEXT TYPEFACE: *Various* CLIENT: *Mead Fine Paper Division*

63 DESIGN FIRM: *Peterson & Company* DESIGNER: *Bryan L. Peterson* HEADLINE TYPEFACE: *Various* TEXT TYPEFACE: *Various*

66

64 DESIGN FIRM: Peterson & Company   DESIGNER: Bryan L. Peterson   HEADLINE TYPEFACE: Various   TEXT TYPEFACE: Various   CLIENT: Mead Fine Paper Division

65 DESIGN FIRM: Segura Inc.   DESIGNER: Carlos Segura   LETTERER: Carlos Segura   HEADLINE TYPEFACE: Letter   TCLIENT: The Merchandise Mart

66 DESIGN FIRM: Thirst/Chicago   DESIGNER: Rick Valicenti, Mark Rattin and Tony Klassen   HEADLINE TYPEFACE: Meta   TEXT TYPEFACE: Swift   CLIENT: The Color Center

**67**

New Haven Line
Effective October 15, 1992

# Southport
# Freight
# Station

Southport, Connecticut ♿

**H** **Roger Huyssen**
**Gerard Huerta**
**2H Studio**

Information:
54 Old Post Road
Southport, CT 06490
FAX: (203) 256-1643

Roger Huyssen:
(203) 256-9192
Gerard Huerta:
(203) 256-1625

### We've moved...

To a new location at the Southport Freight Station. Please make a note of our new phones, fax and address.

Roger Huyssen is still right on track with his many Time covers, movie art, Super Bowl '93 poster and a variety of advertising and product illustrations for which he's well known.

Gerard Huerta can engineer a logo, typographic illustration or meet all your handlettering needs with on-time express service.

As 2H Studio we've collaborated to give our clients first-class service. For a quick sampling refer to American Showcase Illustration back flaps Volumes 13, 14, 15 and 16.

The Southport Freight Station: your stop for all of your art needs.

**68**

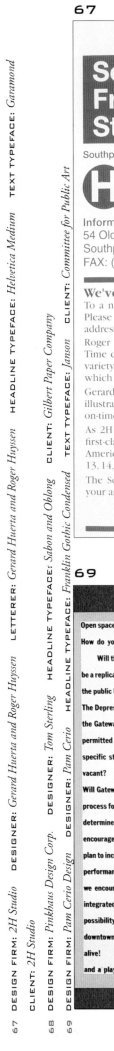

**69**

Open spaces in Gateway should allow people to relax in a setting that's full of trees, benches, water and art. How do you propose to create this environment when stadiums in the past have focused on parking? Will the design of the baseball stadium have a unique flavor that reflects the City of Cleveland or will it be a replica of the new Baltimore and Comiskey Ballparks? Typically, the budget is never enough to build the public buildings the community wants. Granite was proposed for City Hall but it was built of limestone. The Depression forced the existing stadium to be faced with brick. What materials are you considering for the Gateway stadium and arena? How will existing merchants in the area, who also own property, be permitted to restrict the future development, in terms of design, i.e., height limits, facade, etc.? What specific steps has the city taken to ensure the preservation of all the existing structures--occupied or vacant? What impact will Gateway have on the patrons who now shop in the E. 4th shopping district? Will Gateway remain sensitive to the social make-up of the area? Have you envisioned or planned the process for determining the "flavor of Cleveland?" What individuals do you see as being the ones who might determine this? Is it possible to design the stadium and the arena with acoustics good enough to encourage the scheduling of rock, pop, and country concerts throughout much of the year? Is there any plan to incorporate the performing arts in any of these spaces, either as permanent tenants or for occasional performances? I am worried about parking lots--they are like magnets for historic buildings. How can we encourage fewer parking lots--get people to take public transportation? If the project is to be integrated into the city, we need to retain/expand the pedestrian environment. Please comment on the possibility of providing additional walkways to encourage walking and the use of public transportation to downtown. Please no pedestrian tunnels and no bridges--keep the people on the street to keep the city alive! I would encourage a parklike setting around the 2 buildings which would provide areas for picnics, and a playground. These facilities could be used year round. What about the use of bicycle paths?

Designing Gateway:
Work to Date

*a public forum*

**TIME FOR ANOTHER OUTPUT OF PUBLIC INPUT!** It's **YOUR** continuing input that will help make Gateway uniquely Cleveland. **DURING OUR FIRST PROGRAM,** you asked such questions as, "How is the Gateway Project Development Team going to respond to ideas?" And, "Can the Team really integrate the public's thinking into this large development scheme and still design a stadium and arena which work?" **So** come one, come all, with questions, comments, suggestions. You'll hear **ANSWERS, INSIGHTS, UPDATES ON GATEWAY,** as master planners, site designers and facility architects present their concepts.

*program*
**(2)**

67 DESIGN FIRM: 2H Studio DESIGNER: Gerard Huyssen and Roger Huyssen LETTERER: Gerard Huyssen and Roger Huyssen HEADLINE TYPEFACE: Helvetica Medium TEXT TYPEFACE: Garamond CLIENT: 2H Studio

68 DESIGN FIRM: Pinkhaus Design Corp. DESIGNER: Tom Sterling HEADLINE TYPEFACE: Sabon and Oblong TEXT TYPEFACE: Janson CLIENT: Gilbert Paper Company

69 DESIGN FIRM: Pam Cerio Design DESIGNER: Pam Cerio HEADLINE TYPEFACE: Franklin Gothic Condensed CLIENT: Committee for Public Art

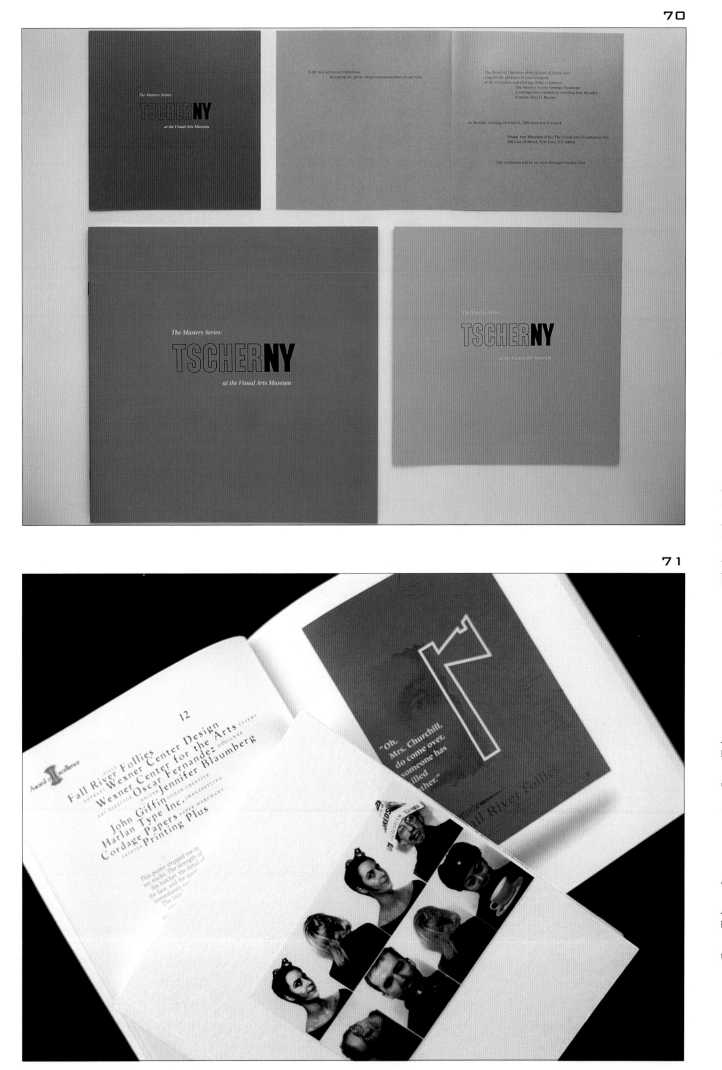

70  **DESIGN FIRM:** *George Tscherny, Inc.*  **DESIGNER:** *George Tscherny*  **HEADLINE TYPEFACE:** *Whedons Gothic Outline*  **TEXT TYPEFACE:** *Walbaum*  **CLIENT:** *Visual Arts Museum*

71  **DESIGN FIRM:** *Schmeltz + Warren*  **DESIGNER:** *Crit Warren/Dave Bennett*  **HEADLINE TYPEFACE:** *F: Alphabet*  **TEXT TYPEFACE:** *F: FloMotion/F: Scratched Out*  **CLIENT:** *Columbus Society of Communicating Arts*

**72**

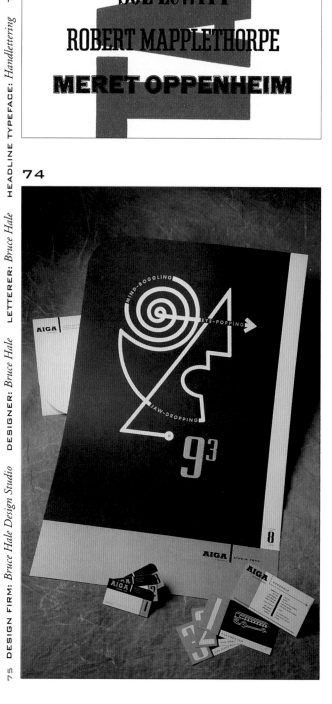

SCOTT BURTON
BRYAN HUNT
NEIL JENNEY
RONALD JONES
DONALD JUDD
YVES KLEIN
WIN KNOWLTON
SOL LeWITT
ROBERT MAPPLETHORPE
MERET OPPENHEIM

**73**

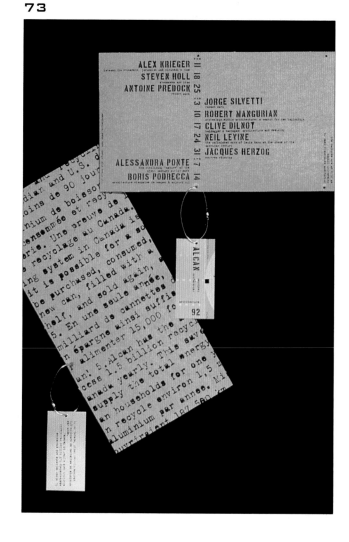

ALEX KRIEGER
STEVEN HOLL
ANTOINE PREDOCK
JORGE SILVETTI
ROBERT MANGURIAN
CLIVE DILNOT
NEIL LEVINE
JACQUES HERZOG
ALESSANDRA PONTE
BORIS PODRECCA

**74**

**75**

MIND-BOGGLING
EYE-POPPING
JAW-DROPPING
9³

AIGA

when our store lights are switched off
this Christmas Eve a Warmth will Linger

Merry Christmas
from The Bon Marche

The BON MARCHÉ

---

72 TEXT TYPEFACE: Hellenic Wide, Astoria, Tower, Onyx and Railroad Gothic   CLIENT: A/D Gallery

73 TEXT TYPEFACE: Antique Typewriter   TEXT TYPEFACE: Antique Stencils   CLIENT: Alcan Aluminum Ltd.

74 TEXT TYPEFACE: Futura   CLIENT: AIGA/Minnesota

75 TEXT TYPEFACE: Handlettering   CLIENT: The Bon Marche

72 HEADLINE TYPEFACE: Gothic Wood Type   DESIGNER: Peter Kruty

73 HEADLINE TYPEFACE: Antique Typewriter   DESIGNER: Anita Meyer, Jan Baker, Matthew Monk

74 HEADLINE TYPEFACE: Memphis and Thick and Thin Gaspipe   DESIGNER: Joel Templin

75 HEADLINE TYPEFACE: Handlettering   LETTERER: Bruce Hale   DESIGNER: Bruce Hale

72 DESIGN FIRM: Peter Kruty Editions

73 DESIGN FIRM: plus design inc.

74 DESIGN FIRM: Gardner Design

75 DESIGN FIRM: Bruce Hale Design Studio

76 DESIGN FIRM: *Segura Inc.*   DESIGNER: *Carlos Segura*   LETTERER: *Carlos Segura*   HEADLINE TYPEFACE: *Keedy/Arbitrary*   TEXT TYPEFACE: *Keedy/Arbitrary*   CLIENT: *How Design Conference*

**77**

**78**

77 **DESIGN FIRM:** *Schmeltz + Warren*    **DESIGNER:** *Crit Warren*    **HEADLINE TYPEFACE:** *Bell Gothic*    **TEXT TYPEFACE:** *Bell Gothic and Alternate Gothic*    **CLIENT:** *Columbus Society of Communicating Arts*

78 **DESIGN FIRM:** *Schmeltz + Warren*    **DESIGNER:** *Crit Warren*    **HEADLINE TYPEFACE:** *Template Gothic*    **TEXT TYPEFACE:** *Egyptian 710, Humanist 970, Egiziano Black and Egyptienne*

**CLIENT:** *The Ohio College Association*

79 DESIGN FIRM: plus design inc.   DESIGNER: Anita Meyer   LETTERER: Jan Baker   CLIENT: The Getty Center for the History of Art and the Humanities

80 DESIGN FIRM: Newell and Sorrell   DESIGNER: Simon Wright and Lin Wong   LETTERER: Cheryl Briggs and Simon Wright   HEADLINE TYPEFACE: Handlettering   CLIENT: Royal Mail

81

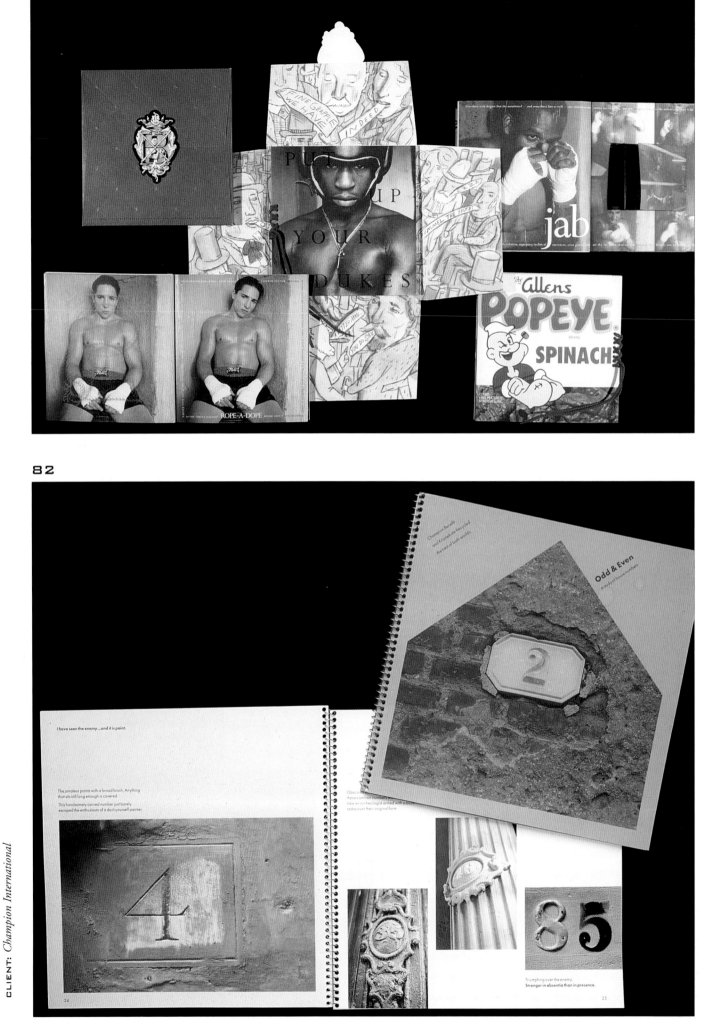

81 DESIGN FIRM: *Robert Valentine Incorporated* DESIGNER: *Robert Valentine and Wayne Wolf* HEADLINE TYPEFACE: *Perpetua* TEXT TYPEFACE: *Perpetua* CLIENT: *Gilbert Paper Company*

82 DESIGN FIRM: *George Tscherny, Inc.* DESIGNER: *George Tscherny, Michelle Novak and Steve Tomkiewicz* HEADLINE TYPEFACE: *Futura Bold* TEXT TYPEFACE: *Futura Book*

CLIENT: *Champion International*

83  DESIGN FIRM: *Stoltze Design*    DESIGNER: *Bob Beerman and Clifford Stoltze*    HEADLINE TYPEFACE: *Monotype Grotesque*    TEXT TYPEFACE: *Franklin Gothic*    CLIENT: *Northeastern University*

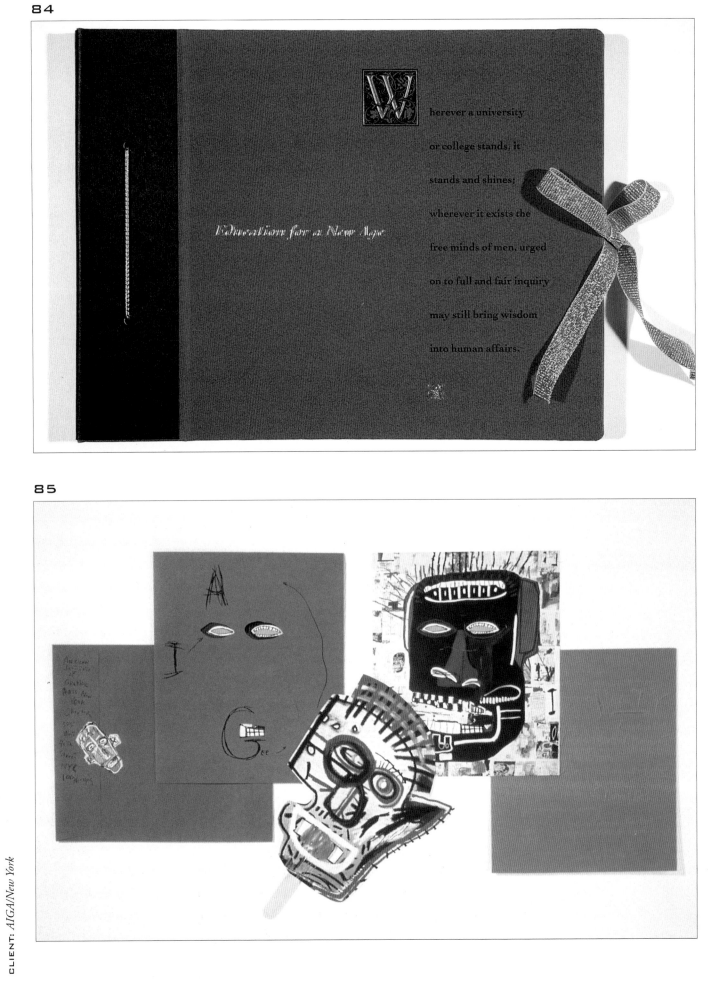

84

85

84 DESIGN FIRM: *Visual Asylum* DESIGNER: *Mae Lin Levine* HEADLINE TYPEFACE: *Caslon Caps* TEXT TYPEFACE: *Cochin Bold and Italic* CLIENT: *Esther LaPorta/USD*

85 DESIGN FIRM: *Robert Valentine Incorporated* DESIGNER: *Robert Valentine and Dina Dell-Arciprete* HEADLINE TYPEFACE: *Handlettering* TEXT TYPEFACE: *Handlettering* LETTERER: *Robert Valentine*

CLIENT: *AIGA/New York*

86

87

86 DESIGN FIRM: *Samata Associates*   DESIGNER: *Pat and Greg Samata*   HEADLINE TYPEFACE: *Orator Bold*   TEXT TYPEFACE: *Orator*   CLIENT: *Simpson Paper Co.*

87 DESIGN FIRM: *Rigsby Design, Inc.*   DESIGNER: *Lana Rigsby and Troy S. Ford*   HEADLINE TYPEFACE: *Futura Extrabold Cond.*   TEXT TYPEFACE: *Century Old Style*   CLIENT: *The Zoological Society of Houston*

88

89

88 DESIGN FIRM: *Patricia Bruning Design* DESIGNER: *Patricia Bruning* TEXT TYPEFACE: *Garamond* CLIENT: *Oakland Museum*

89 DESIGN FIRM: *Pinkhaus Design Corp.* DESIGNER: *Claudia DeCastro and Joel Fuller* TEXT & HEADLINE TYPEFACE: *Caslon Openface* LETTERER: *Claudia DeCastro* TEXT TYPEFACE: *Gill Sans*

CLIENT: *Potlatch Corporation*

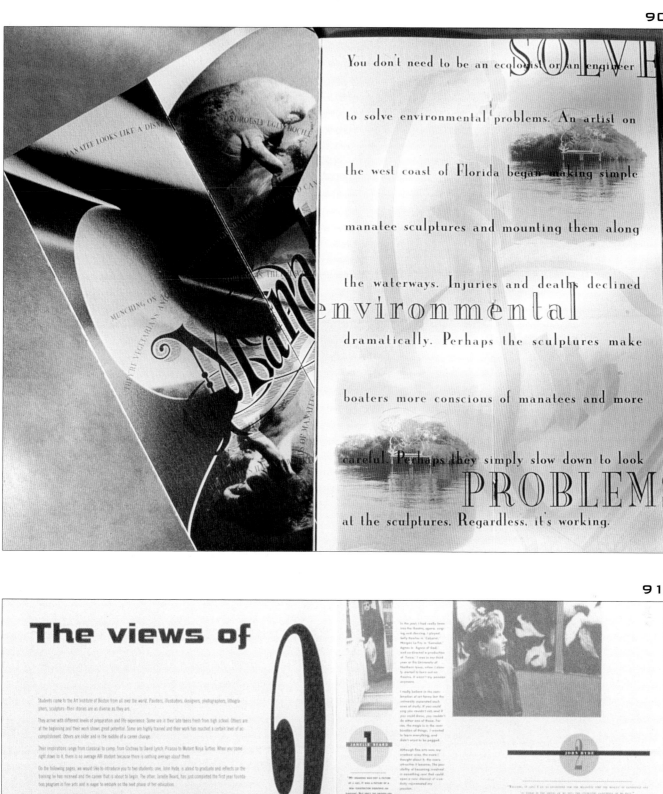

You don't need to be an ecologist or an engineer to solve environmental problems. An artist on the west coast of Florida began making simple manatee sculptures and mounting them along the waterways. Injuries and deaths declined dramatically. Perhaps the sculptures make boaters more conscious of manatees and more careful. Perhaps they simply slow down to look at the sculptures. Regardless, it's working.

**SOLVE** *environmental* **PROBLEMS**

# The views of

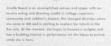

**students**

90  DESIGN FIRM: *Pinkhaus Design Corp.*  DESIGNER: *Tom Sterling*  HEADLINE TYPEFACE: *New Yorker Engraved*  CLIENT: *Gilbert Paper Company*

91  DESIGN FIRM: *Stoltze Design*  DESIGNER: *Clifford Stoltze, Kyong Choe and Carol Sly*  TEXT & HEADLINE TYPEFACE: *Trade Gothic, Franklin Gothic, Futura and Bodoni*  CLIENT: *Art Institute of Boston*

92 DESIGN FIRM: *Hornall Anderson Design Works*   DESIGNER: *Jack Anderson and Heidi Hatlisted*   HEADLINE TYPEFACE: *Custom*   TEXT TYPEFACE: *Palatino*   CLIENT: *Print Northwest*

93 DESIGN FIRM: *Tom Fowler, Inc.*   DESIGNER: *Thomas G. Fowler*   LETTERER: *Thomas G. Fowler*   HEADLINE TYPEFACE: *Handlettering*   TEXT TYPEFACE: *Handlettering*   CLIENT: *Tom Fowler, Inc.*

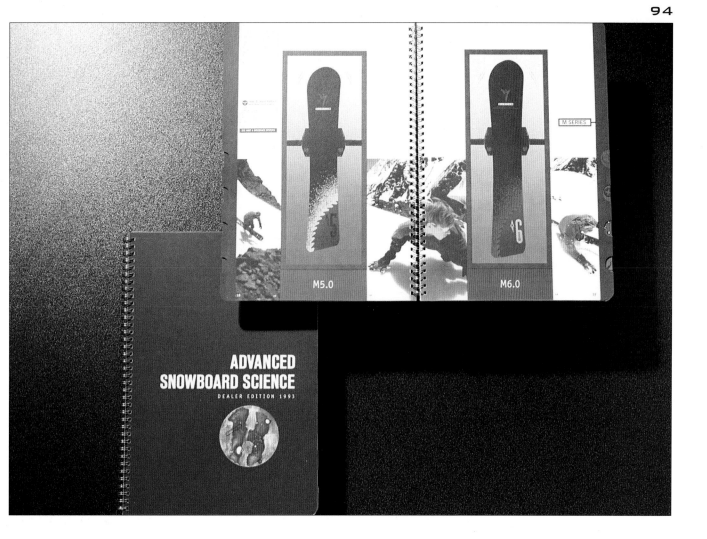

94   **DESIGN FIRM:** Jager DiPaola Kemp Design   **DESIGNER:** David Covell and Adam Levite   **HEADLINE TYPEFACE:** News Gothic   **TEXT TYPEFACE:** Officina   **CLIENT:** Burton Snowboards

95   **DESIGN FIRM:** Emerson, Wajdowicz Studios, Inc.   **DESIGNER:** Jurek Wajdowicz   **HEADLINE TYPEFACE:** Akzidenz Grotesk and Franklin Gothic   **TEXT TYPEFACE:** Gill Sans and Helvetica

**CLIENT:** Emerson, Wajdowicz Studios, Inc.

POSTERS

1  DESIGN FIRM: *Landor Associates*  DESIGNER: *Margaret Youngblood and Doug Becker*  LETTERER: *Margaret Youngblood*  CLIENT: *SF Film Society*

1

When you want to work
hard, we make it easy.

RULE # *8*

**KAPLAN RULES**

Kaplan and only Kaplan has
centers. These are comfortable
places where you can come
and find staff, students,
libraries, tapes, practice tests.
If you start our course in
Michigan, you can finish it in
Hawaii. If you miss a class,
you can make it up. Days,
evenings, weekends.

# Convenience is

**KAPLAN** *The answer to the test question*

2  DESIGN FIRM: *Parham Santana Inc.*  DESIGNER: *Alexander Knowlton and Jaqueline Thaw*  HEADLINE TYPEFACE: *Bauer Bodoni/Swiss 921*  TEXT TYPEFACE: *Bodoni and Kuenstler Script*  CLIENT: *Kaplan*

3  **DESIGN FIRM:** *Michael Schwab Design*  **DESIGNER:** *Michael Schwab*  **LETTERER:** *Michael Schwab*  **HEADLINE TYPEFACE:** *Plakastil Poster Style*  **CLIENT:** *San Francisco Opera*

**4**

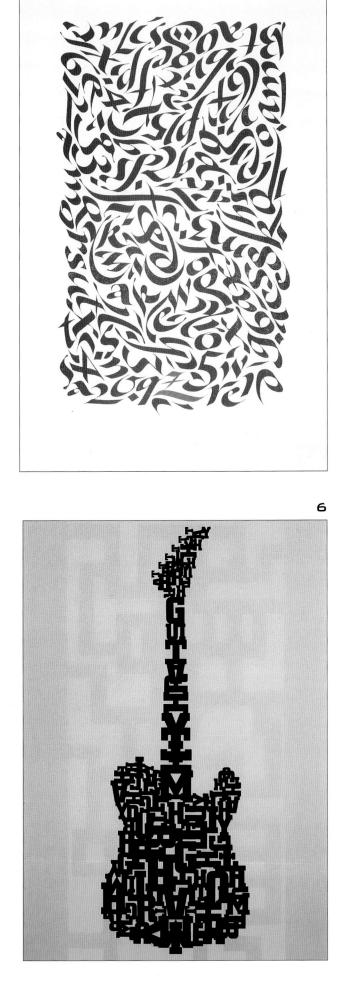

**5**

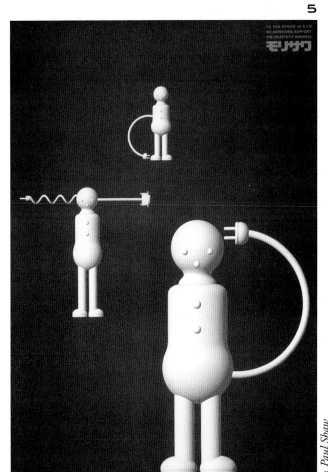

**6**

**7**

8   DESIGN FIRM: *Richard Poulin Design Group Inc.*   DESIGNER: *Richard Poulin*   HEADLINE TYPEFACE: *Walbaum and City*   CLIENT: *Association of Independent Commercial Producers*

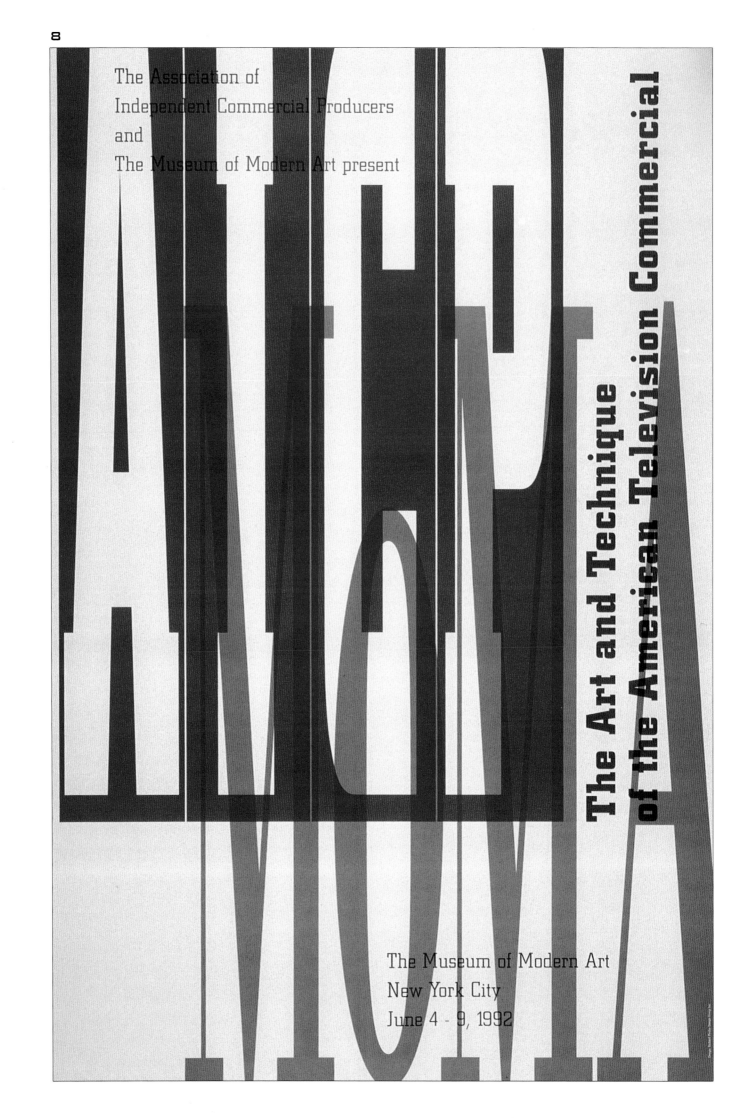

The Association of
Independent Commercial Producers
and
The Museum of Modern Art present

**The Art and Technique
of the American Television Commercial**

The Museum of Modern Art
New York City
June 4 - 9, 1992

AIGA
NEW YORK
BEHIND
THE
WHEEL
FRESH DIALOGUE
JUNE 5
1991
7PM
KATIE
MURPHY
AMPHITHEATRE
FIT

JENNIFER
MORLA
MORLA
DESIGN
SAN FRANCISCO
CHIP
KIDD
KNOPF
NYC
JILLY
SIMONS
CONCRETE
CHICAGO

9  DESIGN FIRM: *Richard Poulin Design Group Inc.*  DESIGNER: *Richard Poulin*  HEADLINE TYPEFACE: *Franklin Gothic*  CLIENT: *AIGA/NY*

11

12

11  DESIGN FIRM: *The Leonhardt Group*  DESIGNER: *Jon Cannell*  LETTERER: *Jon Cannell*  HEADLINE TYPEFACE: *Univers*  TEXT TYPEFACE: *Univers*  CLIENT: *Seafair*

12  DESIGN FIRM: *Landor Associates*  DESIGNER: *Margaret Youngblood and Rachel Wear*  LETTERER: *Rachel Wear*  CLIENT: *SF Film Society*

**13 DESIGN FIRM:** *Kan Tai-keung Design & Associates Ltd.* **DESIGNER:** *Kan Tai-keung* **HEADLINE TYPEFACE:** *Chinese: Gothic / English: Univers* **CLIENT:** *Hong Kong Artists' Guild*

THE FIFTH ASIAN

INTERNATIONAL ART EXHIBITION

DECEMBER 15, 1990 — JANUARY 6, 1991

NATIONAL ART GALLERY, MALAYSIA

第五屆亞洲國際美術展覽

九零年十二月十五日至九一年一月六日

馬來西亞國家藝術館

14 DESIGN FIRM: *Kan Tai-keung Design & Associates Ltd.* DESIGNER: *Kan Tai-keung* HEADLINE TYPEFACE: *Gill Sans* CLIENT: *Kan Tai-keung Design & Associates Ltd.*

**15**

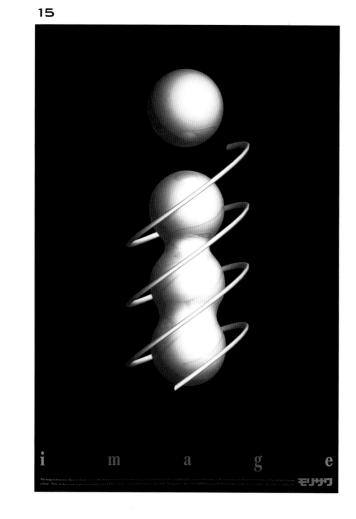

**16**

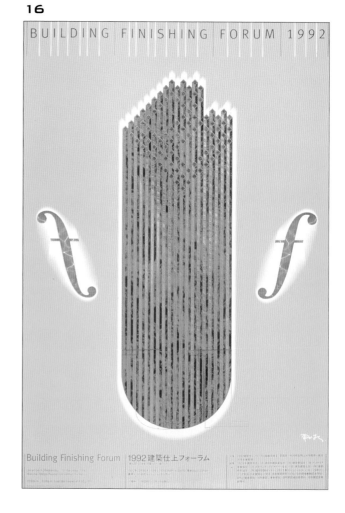

**17**

15 DESIGN FIRM: *Packaging Create Inc.* DESIGNER: *Shuichi Nogami* LETTERER: *Shuichi Nogami* HEADLINE TYPEFACE: *Original* TEXT TYPEFACE: *Times Bold* CLIENT: *Morisawa & Company, Ltd.*

16 DESIGN FIRM: *M Plus M Inc.* DESIGNER: *Takaaki Matsumoto* CLIENT: *Building Finishing Forum*

17 DESIGN FIRM: *M Plus M Inc.* DESIGNER: *Takaaki Matsumoto* CLIENT: *AIGA*

18  DESIGN FIRM: *246 Fifth Design Inc.*  DESIGNER: *Terry Laurenzio and Sid Lee*  HEADLINE TYPEFACE: *Bergell*  TEXT TYPEFACE: *Retro Bold*  CLIENT: *Ottawa Jazz Festival, Inc.*

19

19 DESIGN FIRM: *Peterson & Company* DESIGNER: *Scott Ray* LETTERER: *Scott Ray and Lynn Rowe Reed* HEADLINE TYPEFACE: *Hand lettering* TEXT TYPEFACE: *Hand lettering*

CLIENT: *Garland Performing Arts Center*

DESIGN FIRM: *Tharp Did It*  DESIGNER: *Rick Tharp and Colleen Sullivan*  LETTERER: *Smith Corona*  HEADLINE TYPEFACE: *Elite*  TEXT TYPEFACE: *Elite*  CLIENT: *Tharp Did It*

20  DESIGN FIRM: *Tharp Did It*  DESIGNER: *Rick Tharp and Colleen Sullivan*  LETTERER: *Smith Corona*

**21**
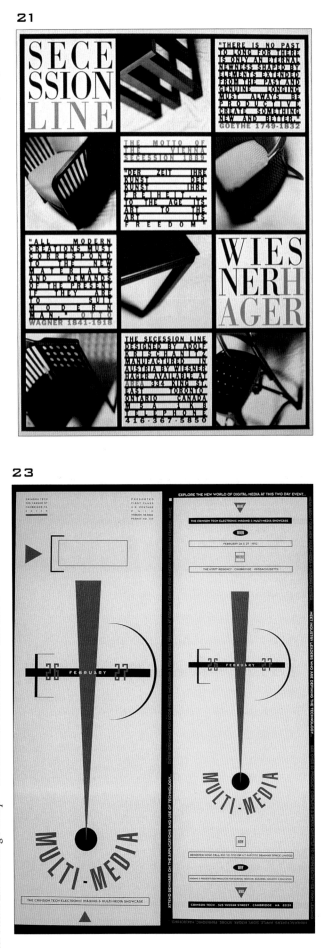

**22**

**23**
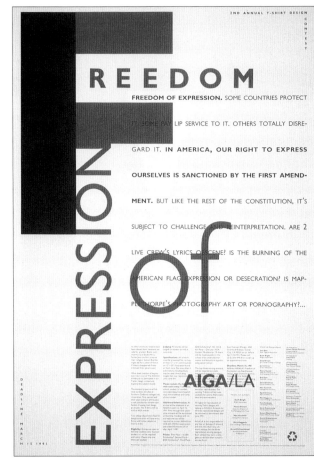

**24**

25  DESIGN FIRM: *Muller & Company*  DESIGNER: *John Muller and Scott Chapman*  LETTERER: *John Muller*  CLIENT: *K. C. Jazz Commission*

26  DESIGN FIRM: *Graffito*  DESIGNER: *Dave Plunkert*  HEADLINE TYPEFACE: *Grand B*  TEXT TYPEFACE: *Meta Bold*  CLIENT: *Intelsat*

### Glynn Williams
# My own sculpture
*and its relationship to site*

Glynn Williams, one of Britain's leading contemporary stone sculptors presents a retrospective glimpse of his work over twenty-five years. He is currently Professor of Sculpture at the Royal College of Art with much of his work included in an impressive list of public collections such as the Tate Gallery, and Hakone Open-Air Museum, Japan.

The lecture will take place at Pentagram Design, 11 Needham Road, London W11 2RP on Wednesday, 21 October at 6.30 for 7.00pm. The nearest tube is Notting Hill Gate. Admission is free for members, £2.50 for non-members. For further information contact Coralie Langston-Jones on 071 792 3812.

## Educating for the Percent for Art

Art & Architecture/Royal College of Art Forum.
As the Percent for Art campaign gains momentum, what role should schools of art and architecture play? Join in this lively discussion at the Royal College of Art, Main Lecture Theatre, 30th October 1991, 6.30pm. Admission free. For further information contact Mairead McClements at the RCA. Telephone 071 584 5020.

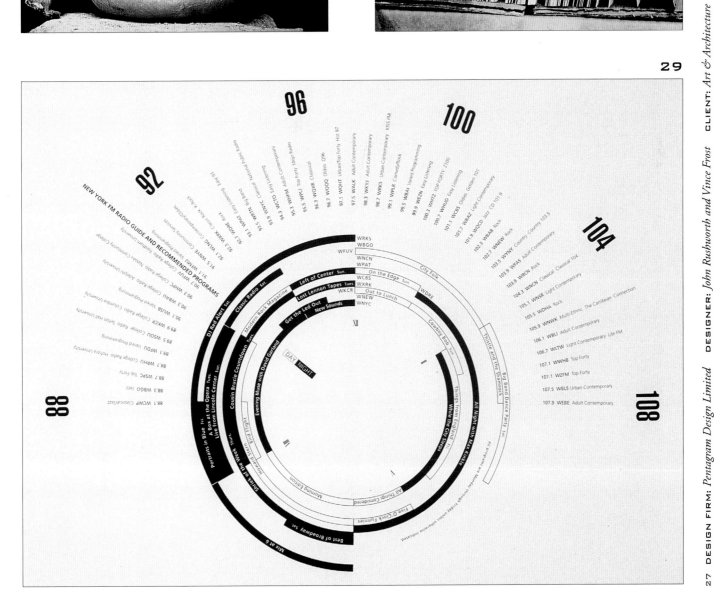

NEW YORK FM RADIO GUIDE AND RECOMMENDED PROGRAMS

27  **DESIGN FIRM:** *Pentagram Design Limited*  **DESIGNER:** *John Rushworth and Vince Frost*  **CLIENT:** *Art & Architecture*

28  **DESIGN FIRM:** *Pentagram Design Limited*  **DESIGNER:** *John Rushworth and Vince Frost*  **CLIENT:** *Art & Architecture*

29  **DESIGN FIRM:** *Vincent Lisi*  **DESIGNER:** *Vincent Lisi*  **HEADLINE TYPEFACE:** *Helvetica Ultra Compressed and Frutiger 65*  **TEXT TYPEFACE:** *Frutiger 55 Roman and Frutiger 45 Light*  **CLIENT:** *Vincent Lisi*

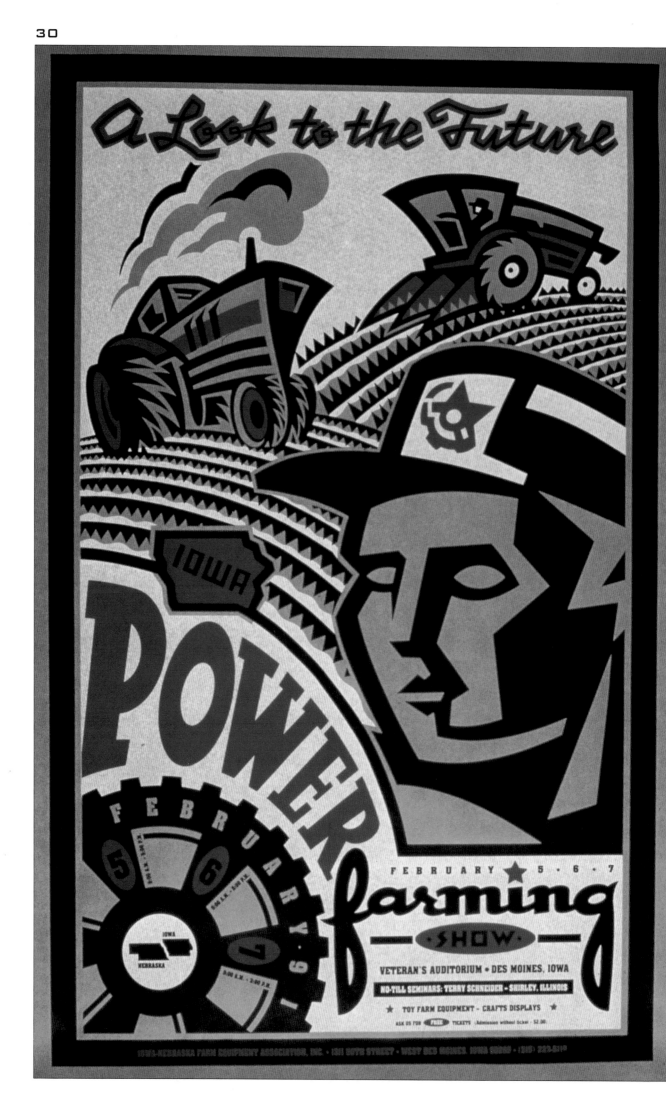

30 DESIGN FIRM: *Sayles Graphic Design* DESIGNER: *John Sayles* LETTERER: *John Sayles* HEADLINE TYPEFACE: *Handlettering* TEXT TYPEFACE: *Aachen Bold*

CLIENT: *Iowa-Nebraska Farm Equipment Association*

31 DESIGN FIRM: *Sayles Graphic Design* DESIGNER: *John Sayles* LETTERER: *John Sayles* HEADLINE TYPEFACE: *Handlettering* TEXT TYPEFACE: *Typewritten* CLIENT: *Associated General Contractors*

32

32 DESIGN FIRM: *Sayles Graphic Design*   DESIGNER: *John Sayles*   LETTERER: *John Sayles*   HEADLINE TYPEFACE: *Handlettering*   TEXT TYPEFACE: *Handlettering*   CLIENT: *RAGBRAI XX*

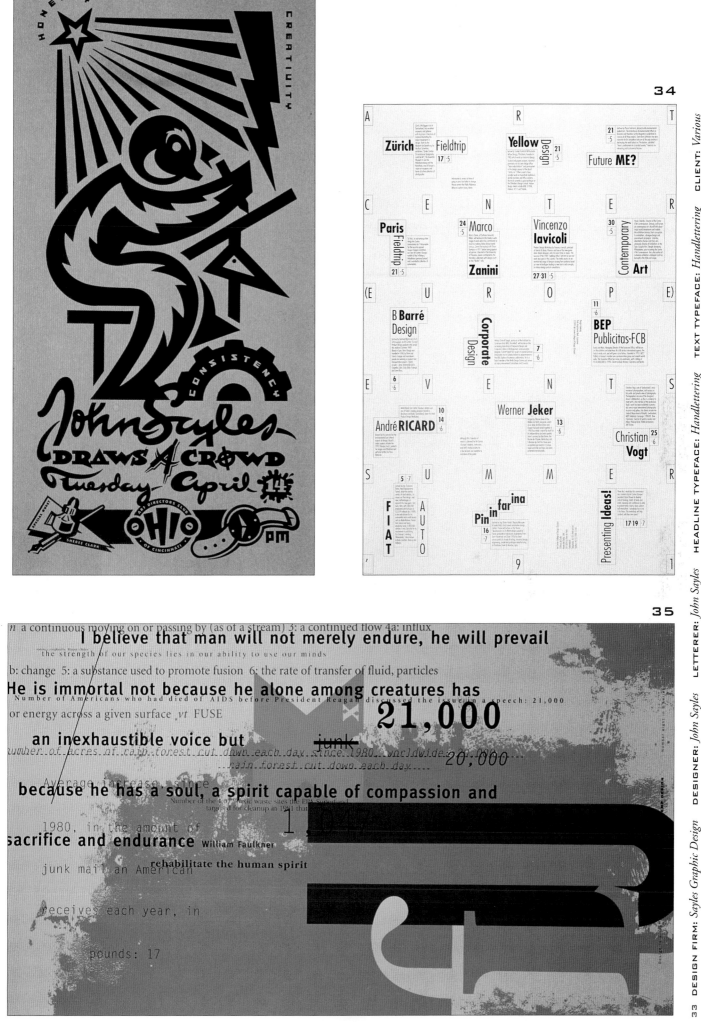

33  DESIGN FIRM: *Sayles Graphic Design*  DESIGNER: *John Sayles*  LETTERER: *John Sayles*  HEADLINE TYPEFACE: *Handlettering*  TEXT TYPEFACE: *Handlettering*  CLIENT: *Various*

34  DESIGN FIRM: *Looking*  DESIGNER: *John Clark*  HEADLINE TYPEFACE: *Looking*  TEXT TYPEFACE: *Meta and Letter Gothic*  CLIENT: *Art Center College of Design (Europe)*

35  DESIGN FIRM: *Jager DiPaola Kemp Design*  DESIGNER: *Janet Johnson, Dan Sharp and Steve Bowman*  TEXT TYPEFACE: *Meta and Letter Gothic*  CLIENT: *Jager DiPaola Kemp Design*

36  DESIGN FIRM: *Mark Oliver, Inc.*   DESIGNER: *Mark Oliver*   HEADLINE TYPEFACE: *Stone Sans Bold*   TEXT TYPEFACE: *Futura Bold*   CLIENT: *Firestone Vineyard*

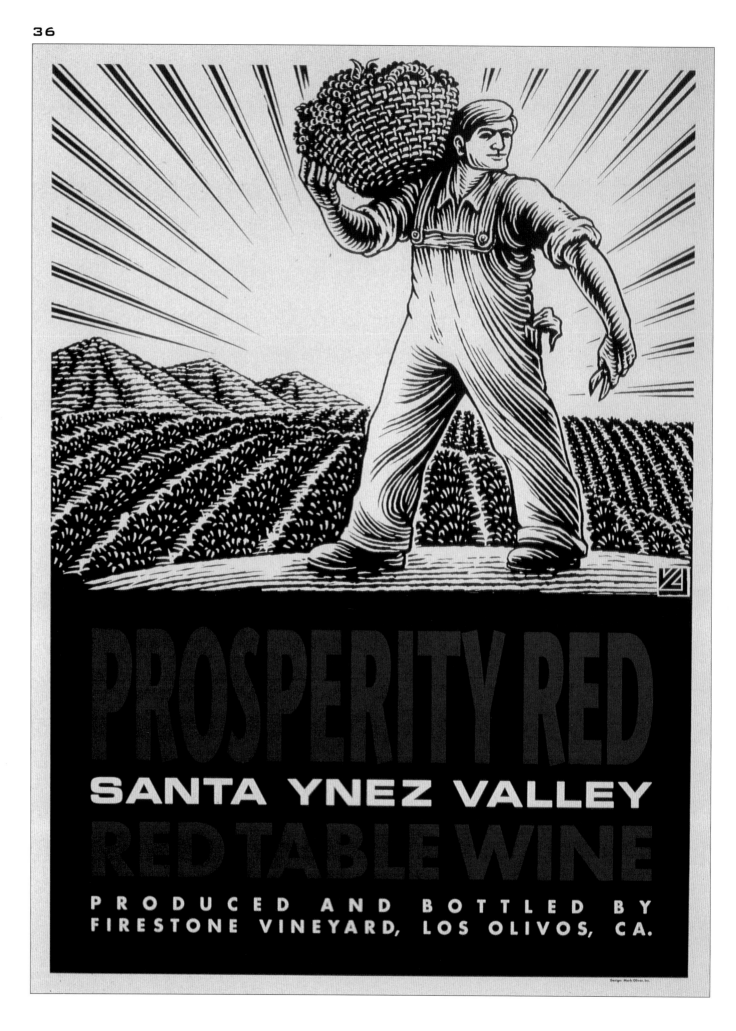

I'm here.

The JAGDA Peace and Environment Poster Exhibition "I'm here."

37 DESIGN FIRM: Taste Inc.   DESIGNER: Toshiyasu Nanbu   LETTERER: Toshiyasu Nanbu   CLIENT: Japan Graphic Designers Association Inc.

38

38 DESIGN FIRM: *Morla Design* DESIGNER: *Jennifer Morla* LETTERER: *Jennifer Morla* HEADLINE TYPEFACE: *Handlettering* TEXT TYPEFACE: *Futura Bold and Extra Bold*

CLIENT: *American Institute of Graphic Arts*

39 DESIGN FIRM: *DesignArt, Inc.* DESIGNER: *Norman Moore* LETTERER: *Norman Moore* HEADLINE TYPEFACE: *Gill* CLIENT: *Capitol Records*

40 DESIGN FIRM: *Dayton's Department Stores* DESIGNER: *Matt Eller* HEADLINE TYPEFACE: *Franklin Gothic Condensed* TEXT TYPEFACE: *Franklin Gothic Condensed* CLIENT: *Ballet of the Dolls*

41 DESIGN FIRM: *Dayton's Department Stores* DESIGNER: *Matt Eller* HEADLINE TYPEFACE: *Egyptienne* TEXT TYPEFACE: *Times Roman and Helvetica Condensed* CLIENT: *Ballet of the Dolls*

40

41

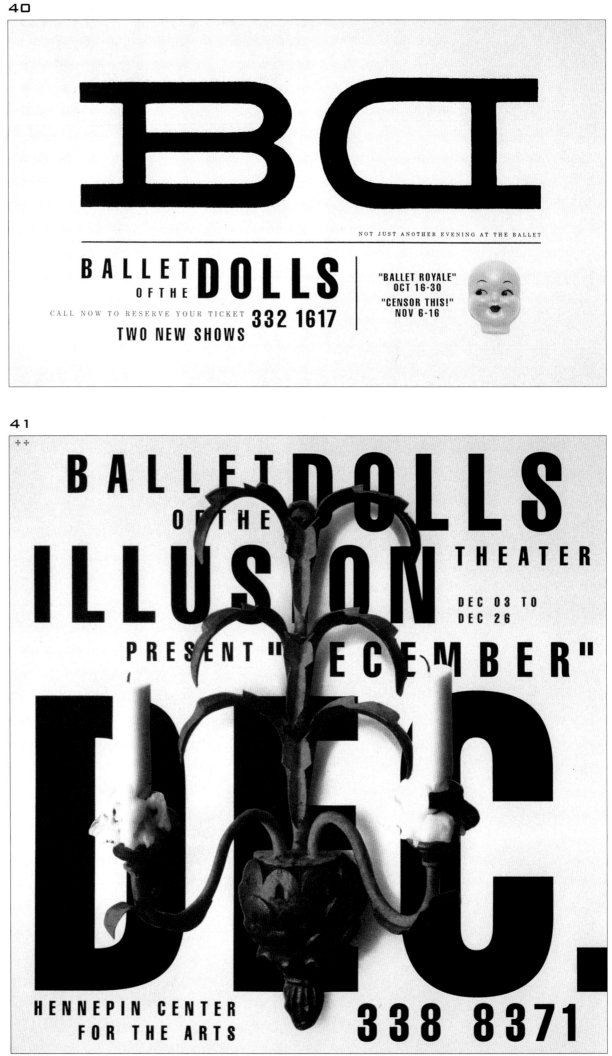

The Columbus Recreation And Parks Depart-

# MUSIC

ment Presents Over 200 Free Outdoor Perfor-

# IN

mances, All In            Our Columbus

Parks From May 22 Through September 18,

# THE

1992. For            Further

Information Call 645-7995. For Performance

# AIR

Listings            Call At

645-3800. It's Quite An Uplifting Experience!

42  DESIGN FIRM: *Rickabaugh Graphics*  DESIGNER: *Eric Rickabaugh*  LETTERER: *Eric Rickabaugh*  HEADLINE TYPEFACE: *Handlettering*  TEXT TYPEFACE: *Linoscript and Futura*

CLIENT: *Columbus Recreation and Parks Department*

43 DESIGN FIRM: *Peterson & Company* DESIGNER: *Bryan L. Peterson* HEADLINE TYPEFACE: *Caslon Openface* TEXT TYPEFACE: *Caslon Openface* CLIENT: *The Friends of the SMU libraries, Colophon*

43

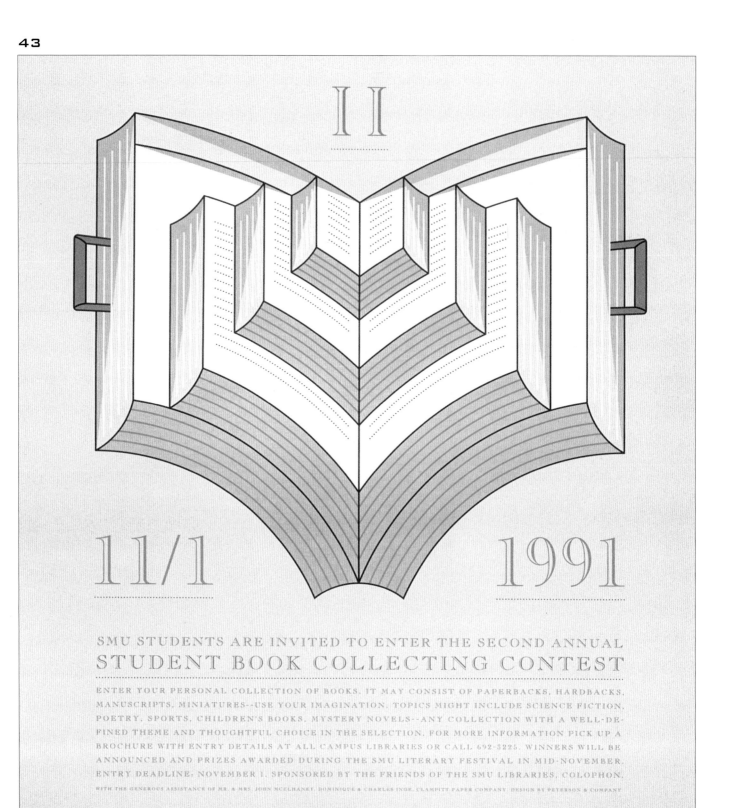

II

11/1                1991

SMU STUDENTS ARE INVITED TO ENTER THE SECOND ANNUAL
STUDENT BOOK COLLECTING CONTEST

ENTER YOUR PERSONAL COLLECTION OF BOOKS. IT MAY CONSIST OF PAPERBACKS, HARDBACKS, MANUSCRIPTS, MINIATURES--USE YOUR IMAGINATION. TOPICS MIGHT INCLUDE SCIENCE FICTION, POETRY, SPORTS, CHILDREN'S BOOKS, MYSTERY NOVELS--ANY COLLECTION WITH A WELL-DEFINED THEME AND THOUGHTFUL CHOICE IN THE SELECTION. FOR MORE INFORMATION PICK UP A BROCHURE WITH ENTRY DETAILS AT ALL CAMPUS LIBRARIES OR CALL 692-5225. WINNERS WILL BE ANNOUNCED AND PRIZES AWARDED DURING THE SMU LITERARY FESTIVAL IN MID-NOVEMBER. ENTRY DEADLINE: NOVEMBER 1. SPONSORED BY THE FRIENDS OF THE SMU LIBRARIES, COLOPHON. WITH THE GENEROUS ASSISTANCE OF MR. & MRS. JOHN MCELHANEY, DOMINIQUE & CHARLES INGE, CLAMPITT PAPER COMPANY. DESIGN BY PETERSON & COMPANY

44

44 DESIGN FIRM: *Marc English: Design*   DESIGNER: *Marc English and Tom Nielsen*   HEADLINE TYPEFACE: *Gill Sans Bold*   TEXT TYPEFACE: *Gill Sans*   CLIENT: *AIGA/Boston*

# P

PACKAGING

**1**

**2**

**3**

**4**

1　DESIGN FIRM: *Hallmark Cards, Inc.*　DESIGNER: *Martha Swords*　LETTERER: *Martha Swords*　HEADLINE TYPEFACE: *Handlettering*　CLIENT: *Hallmark Cards*

2　DESIGN FIRM: *DBD International*　DESIGNER: *David Brier*　LETTERER: *David Brier*　HEADLINE TYPEFACE: *Handlettering*　CLIENT: *Esteé Lauder*

3　DESIGN FIRM: *The Leonhardt Group*　DESIGNER: *Traci Daberkow*　LETTERER: *Nancy Stentz*　HEADLINE TYPEFACE: *Handlettering*　TEXT TYPEFACE: *Cochin*　CLIENT: *Vintage Northwest*

4　DESIGN FIRM: *Lewis Moberly*　DESIGNER: *Mary Lewis*　HEADLINE TYPEFACE: *Perpetua and Handlettering*　TEXT TYPEFACE: *Perpetua and Handlettering*　CLIENT: *Sogrape Vinhos de Portugal*

5   DESIGN FIRM: *Tim Girvin Design, Inc.*   DESIGNER: *Tim Girvin and Theresa Axe*   LETTERER: *Tim Girvin*   HEADLINE TYPEFACE: *Handlettering*   TEXT TYPEFACE: *Univers Ultra Condensed and Futura*

CLIENT: *Alhadeff Distributing Company*

**6**

**7**

**8**

TEXT TYPEFACE: *Univers 57*   CLIENT: *Bass*

CLIENT: *Sogrape Vinhos de Portugal*

HEADLINE TYPEFACE: *Handlettering*   TEXT TYPEFACE: *Gill Extended*   CLIENT: *Inch's Cider*

HEADLINE TYPEFACE: *Handlettering*

HEADLINE TYPEFACE: *Handlettering*   LETTERER: *Garrick Hamm*

DESIGNER: *David Beard*

DESIGNER: *Mary Lewis*

DESIGNER: *Garrick Hamm*

DESIGN FIRM: *Lewis Moberly*

DESIGN FIRM: *Lewis Moberly*

DESIGN FIRM: *Tutssel Lambie-Nairn*

6

7

8

9   DESIGN FIRM: Hornall Anderson Design Works   DESIGNER: Jack Anderson, Mary Hermes and Leo Raymundo   CLIENT: Broadmoor Baker

10  **DESIGN FIRM:** *Jager DiPaola Kemp Design*  **DESIGNER:** *Steve Farrar*  **HEADLINE TYPEFACE:** *Copperplate and New Baskerville*  **TEXT TYPEFACE:** *Ashley Script and Memphis*  **CLIENT:** *White Crow Software*

11  **DESIGN FIRM:** *Newell and Sorrell*  **DESIGNER:** *Mark-Steen Adamson*  **LETTERER:** *Mark-Steen Adamson*  **CLIENT:** *WH Smith*

12  **DESIGN FIRM:** *The Pushpin Group*  **DESIGNER:** *Greg Simpson*  **HEADLINE TYPEFACE:** *Egiziano Initials*  **TEXT TYPEFACE:** *Lightline Gothic*  **CLIENT:** *Ivy Hill Corp.*

**10**

WHITE CROW

**OnAccount**™

QUICK AND

EASY INVOICING

FOR SMALL

BUSINESSES

The **1** minute INVOICE!

FOR THE MACINTOSH®

W H I T E C R O W

**11**

niceday office perforator

niceday

Office Perforator
with Paper Guide
Capacity 1.8mm
Gauge 8cm
3 year guarantee

**12**

**13**

**14**

**15**

13   **DESIGN FIRM:** *Lewis Moberly*   **DESIGNER:** *Lucilla Scrimgeour*   **HEADLINE TYPEFACE:** *Handlettering*   **TEXT TYPEFACE:** *Univers*   **CLIENT:** *Yves Rocher*

14   **DESIGN FIRM:** *Tim Girvin Design, Inc.*   **DESIGNER:** *Tim Girvin*   **LETTERER:** *Tim Girvin*   **HEADLINE TYPEFACE:** *Handlettering*   **CLIENT:** *Estee Lauder*

15   **DESIGN FIRM:** *Ph.D*   **DESIGNER:** *Clive Piercy*   **TEXT TYPEFACE:** *City and Gill Sans*   **CLIENT:** *Elika*

**16**

**17**

16 DESIGN FIRM: *Warner Bros. Records* DESIGNER: *Kim Champagne* LETTERER: *Anthony Kiedis* CLIENT: *Warner Bros. Records* HEADLINE TYPEFACE: *Norman Moore* TEXT TYPEFACE: *Justlefthand* CLIENT: *A & M Records*

17 DESIGN FIRM: *DesignArt, Inc.* DESIGNER: *Norman Moore* LETTERER: *Norman Moore*

18  **DESIGN FIRM:** *Warner Bros. Records*  **DESIGNER:** *Tom Recchion and Michael Stipe*  **LETTERER:** *Ed Rogers*  **CLIENT:** *R.E.M./Athens Ltd.*

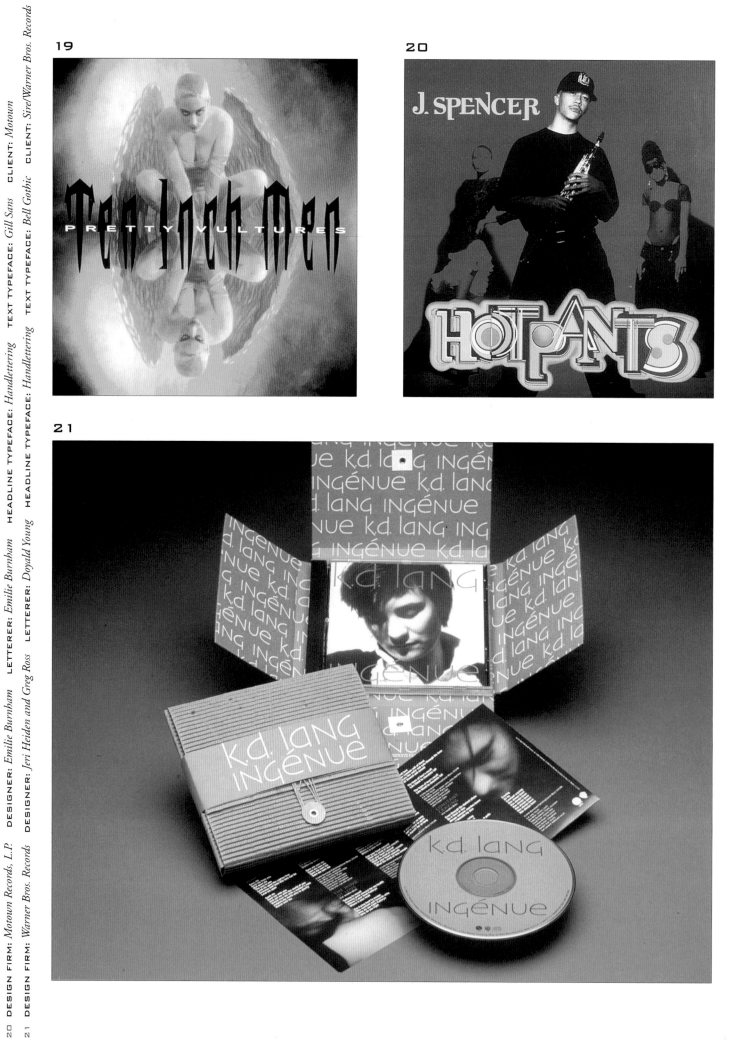

**19**

**20**

**21**

19  DESIGN FIRM: *Margo Chase Design*  DESIGNER: *Margo Chase*  LETTERER: *Margo Chase*  CLIENT: *Victory Music, Inc.*  HEADLINE TYPEFACE: *Handlettering*  TEXT TYPEFACE: *Gill Sans*  CLIENT: *Motown*

20  DESIGN FIRM: *Motown Records, L.P.*  DESIGNER: *Emilie Burnham*  LETTERER: *Emilie Burnham*  HEADLINE TYPEFACE: *Handlettering*  TEXT TYPEFACE: *Bell Gothic*  CLIENT: *Sire/Warner Bros. Records*

21  DESIGN FIRM: *Warner Bros. Records*  DESIGNER: *Jeri Heiden and Greg Ross*  LETTERER: *Doyald Young*

22

23

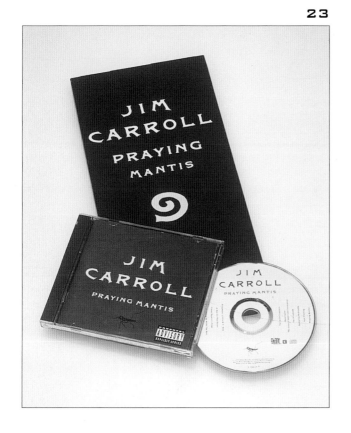

24

22 DESIGN FIRM: *Warner Bros. Records* DESIGNER: *Kim Champagne* CLIENT: *Reprise/Slash Records*

23 DESIGN FIRM: *Warner Bros. Records* DESIGNER: *Henk Elenga* CLIENT: *Giant Records*

24 DESIGN FIRM: *Rey Int'l* DESIGNER: *Jeri Heiden and Kim Champagne* LETTERER: *Michael Rey and Greg Lindey* HEADLINE TYPEFACE: *Handlettering* TEXT TYPEFACE: *Matrix*

CLIENT: *Warner Bros. Records*

**25**

**26**

25 **DESIGN FIRM:** *Independent Project Press*   **DESIGNER:** *Bruce and Karen Licher*   **CLIENT:** *R.E.M./Athens, Ltd.*

26 **DESIGN FIRM:** *Segura Inc.*   **DESIGNER:** *Carlos Segura*   **HEADLINE TYPEFACE:** *Caustic Biomorph*   **CLIENT:** *Synergy Records*

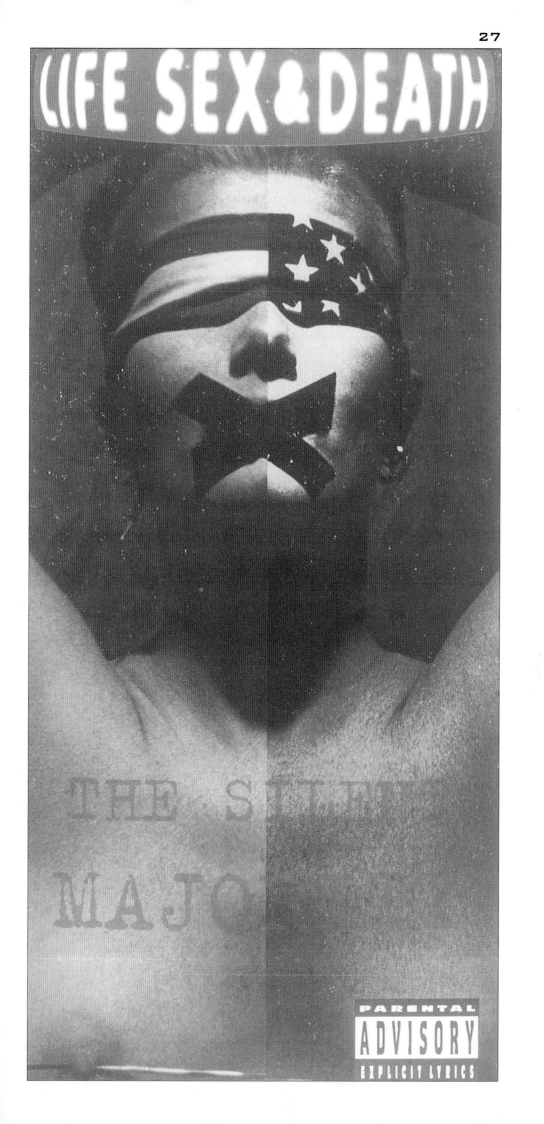

27   **DESIGN FIRM:** *Warner Bros. Records*   **DESIGNER:** *Deborah Norcross, P. Scott Makela and L.S.D.*   **CLIENT:** *Reprise Records*

EDITORIAL

1  DESIGN FIRM: *Carol Publishing Group*  DESIGNER: *Steven Bower*  HEADLINE TYPEFACE: *Futura Bold with Goudy Inline*  TEXT TYPEFACE: *Goudy*  CLIENT: *Carol Publishing Group*

2  DESIGN FIRM: *The Lapis Press*  DESIGNER: *Patrick Dooley*  HEADLINE TYPEFACE: *Bodoni*  TEXT TYPEFACE: *Bodoni*  CLIENT: *The Lapis Press*

3  DESIGN FIRM: *Carol Publishing Group*  DESIGNER: *Steven Bower*  HEADLINE TYPEFACE: *Futura*  TEXT TYPEFACE: *Futura*  CLIENT: *Carol Publishing Group*

**1**

**2**

**3**

# KANJI

SHI
to<u>maru</u>, to<u>meru</u>

STOP!

# PICT·O·GRAPHIX

OVER 1,000 JAPANESE KANJI AND KANA MNEMONICS
Michael Rowley

## 5

MADE IN JAPAN

4  DESIGN FIRM: *Eye Cue Design*  DESIGNER: *Michael Rowley*  LETTERER: *Michael Rowley*  HEADLINE TYPEFACE: *Futura and Handlettering*  TEXT TYPEFACE: *Futura*  CLIENT: *Stone Bridge Press*

5  DESIGN FIRM: *Maureen Erbe Design*  DESIGNER: *Maureen Erbe and Rita Sowins*  HEADLINE TYPEFACE: *Ribbon, Bureau Empire, Raleigh Gothic, Futura Condensed and Hobo*  TEXT TYPEFACE: *Futura Heavy*

CLIENT: *Chronicle Books/San Francisco*

6

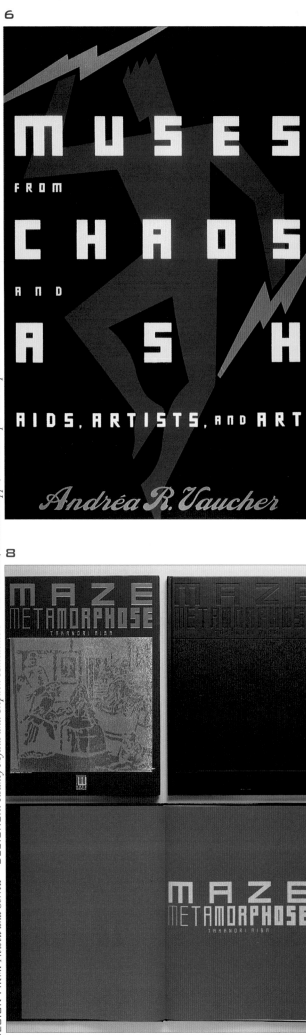

7

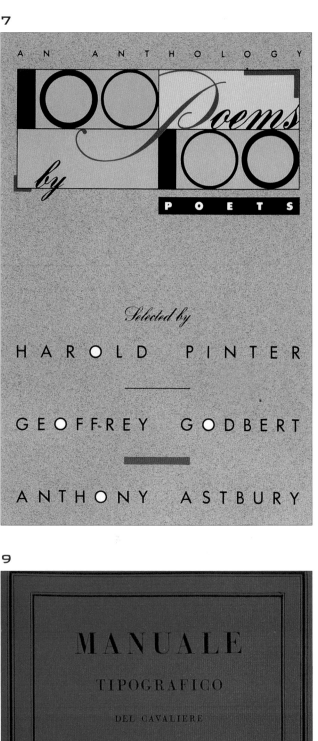

8

9

6    DESIGN FIRM: *Carin Goldberg Design*    DESIGNER: *Carin Goldberg*    HEADLINE TYPEFACE: *Cacucciolo Cubiform (Modified)*    CLIENT: *Grove/Atlantic*

7    DESIGN FIRM: *Carin Goldberg Design*    DESIGNER: *Krystyna Skalski*    HEADLINE TYPEFACE: *Futura and Bank Script*    CLIENT: *Grove/Atlantic*

8    DESIGN FIRM: *Graphics & Designing Inc.*    DESIGNER: *Hiroyuki Hayashi*    LETTERER: *Hiroyuki Hayashi*    CLIENT: *Shinbyoron*

9    DESIGN FIRM: *Newell and Sorrell*    DESIGNER: *Rodney Mylius and Stephen Hutchinson*    LETTERER: *Domenic Lippa, Mark Diaper and Stephen Hutchinson*    HEADLINE TYPEFACE: *Bodoni*

PHOTOGRAPHY & TEXT BY

ANIMA

JAMES BALOG

10  DESIGN FIRM: *Michael Brock Design*  DESIGNER: *Michael Brock and Daina H. Kemp*  HEADLINE TYPEFACE: *Bernhard Modern Roman*  TEXT TYPEFACE: *Bernhard Modern Roman*
CLIENT: *James Balog/Arts Alternative Press*

**11**

FERNANDO MORAIS

*Olga*

REVOLUTIONARY AND MARTYR

**12**

the **I**nsanity of
normality

realism as **sickness**:
toward understanding
**human** destructiveness

arn**o** gruen

**13**

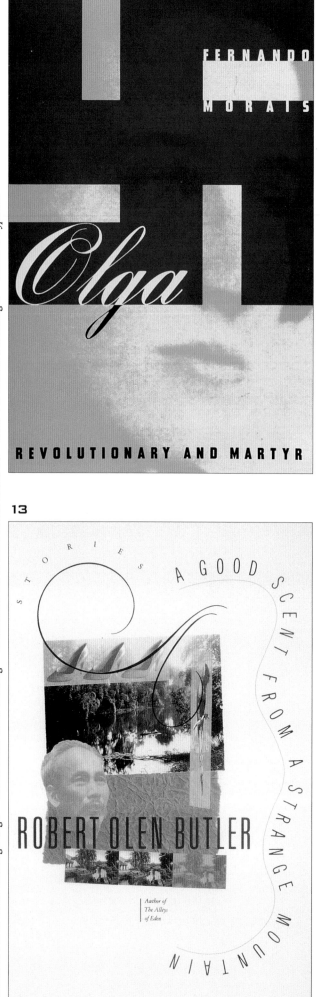

STORIES

A GOOD SCENT FROM A STRANGE MOUNTAIN

ROBERT OLEN BUTLER

*Author of
The Alleys
of Eden*

**14**

b

A NOVEL

o

n

FAE
MYENNE
NG

g

15 DESIGN FIRM: *Carol Publishing Group* DESIGNER: *Steven Bower* HEADLINE TYPEFACE: *Futura Bold Condensed* TEXT TYPEFACE: *Snell Roundhouse and Gothic 820* CLIENT: *Carol Publishing Group*

16   DESIGN FIRM: *Vickie Karten Design*   DESIGNER: *Vickie Sawyer Karten*   HEADLINE TYPEFACE: *Adobe Garamond*   TEXT TYPEFACE: *Adobe Garamond*   CLIENT: *Amateur Athletic Foundation of Los Angeles*

17   DESIGN FIRM: *The Lapis Press*   DESIGNER: *Patrick Dooley*   HEADLINE TYPEFACE: *Bodoni*   TEXT TYPEFACE: *Bodoni*   CLIENT: *The Lapis Press*

**16**

**17**

J.-F. Nicéron
Engraving showing the anamorphic rendering for a wall painting.

The nature of the final product of the series of mirrors depends on a decision about the number, odd or even, of the mirrors. Such is the "solution" that the Socrates of Plato, and later Hegel, proposes for the *dissoi logoi* of the Sophists: the double discourses keep us in a state of incongruence, so we must, says the philosopher, find thirds for them in order to arrive at the unity of contrary theses. You could say the same about circles in motion: a third circle at a tangent to the second will turn in the same direction as the first. The partitions, which are the tangential contacts, are thus two in number: the couple of the specular function and the celibacy of the mirrorish function.

*Bibliography:* Immanuel Kant, *Of the First Foundation of the Difference of Regions in Space* (1768).

### Anamorphoses

A transparent pane of glass can be used as a mirror. Leonardo suggests this to painters, in his *Notebooks:* The object, seen through the pane, is drawn on the glass surface. The drawing is then transferred to an opaque support, set upright like the glass. Now, the two images are congruent superimpositions. However, if you now rotate the pane around a vertical axis and trace the image on the opaque support, the images will not be superimposable. This rotation is the analogue of the mirrorish operation. As you see, the partition functions in two ways: to dissimilate and to assimilate.

The practitioners of perspective refine the specular, or "identitory," function. The machines engraved by

18  DESIGN FIRM: *Adrian Pulfer Design*   DESIGNER: *Adrian Pulfer and Jeff Streeper*   HEADLINE TYPEFACE: *Metro*   TEXT TYPEFACE: *Caslon 540*   CLIENT: *Salt Lake City Winter Olympic Bid Committee*

**19**

"A genuine rarity:
a clever, original idea...
an illuminating lesson."
—Jonathan Yardley

## a day in the night of America
An absorbing journey through the upside-down world of America's night-shift workers
### Kevin Coyne

**20**

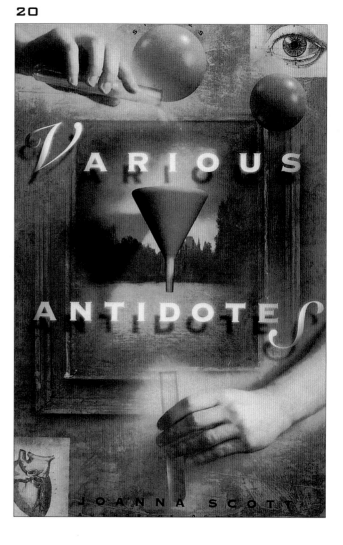

**21**

## ROGER MORRIS
author of *Richard Milhous Nixon: The Rise of an American Politician*

### PROMISES OF
### CHANGE

the clinton

administration

and the politics

of renewal

**22**

19 DESIGN FIRM: *James Victore* DESIGNER: *James Victore* CLIENT: *Henry Holt* HEADLINE TYPEFACE: *Copperplate* TEXT TYPEFACE: *Copperplate* CLIENT: *Henry Holt*

20 DESIGN FIRM: *Richard Tuschman* DESIGNER: *Richard Tuschman* HEADLINE TYPEFACE: *Copperplate* TEXT TYPEFACE: *Futura* CLIENT: *Henry Holt*

21 DESIGN FIRM: *Russell Gordon* DESIGNER: *Russell Gordon* HEADLINE TYPEFACE: *Copperplate* TEXT TYPEFACE: *Futura* CLIENT: *Columbia University Press*

22 DESIGN FIRM: *Carin Goldberg Design* DESIGNER: *Carin Goldberg* HEADLINE TYPEFACE: *Bodoni Book*

23 **DESIGN FIRM:** Carin Goldberg Design **DESIGNER:** Carin Goldberg **HEADLINE TYPEFACE:** Appropriated from a Wienerwerkstatte Poster **CLIENT:** Hyperion

24 DESIGN FIRM: *Carin Goldberg Design*    DESIGNER: *Carin Goldberg*    HEADLINE TYPEFACE: *Eagle Book*    TEXT TYPEFACE: *Metro Black*    CLIENT: *Dell Publishing*

25 DESIGN FIRM: *Carin Goldberg Design*    DESIGNER: *Carin Goldberg*    HEADLINE TYPEFACE: *Eagle Book*    TEXT TYPEFACE: *Metro Black*    CLIENT: *Dell Publishing*

**24**

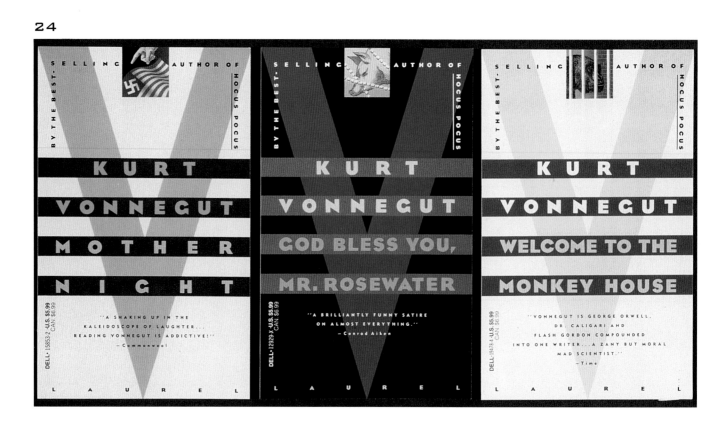

**25**

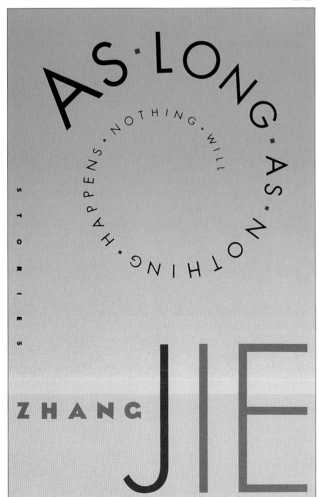

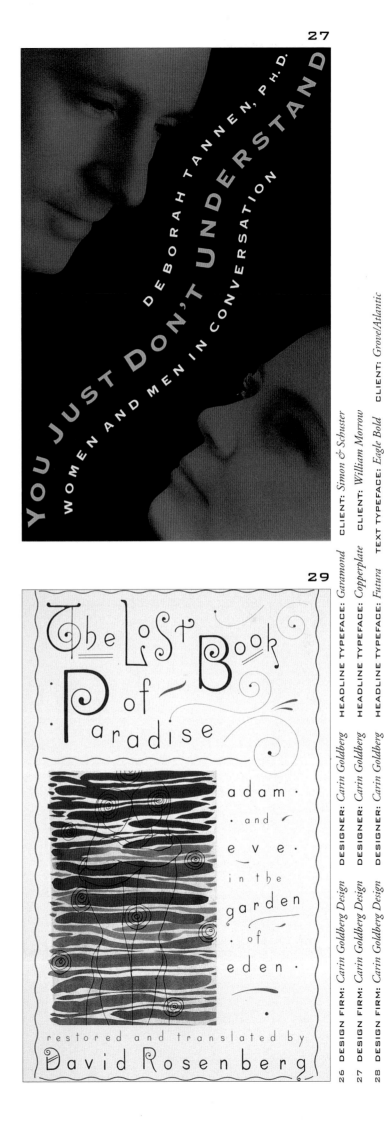

26 DESIGN FIRM: *Carin Goldberg Design*   DESIGNER: *Carin Goldberg*   HEADLINE TYPEFACE: *Garamond*   CLIENT: *Simon & Schuster*

27 DESIGN FIRM: *Carin Goldberg Design*   DESIGNER: *Carin Goldberg*   HEADLINE TYPEFACE: *Copperplate*   CLIENT: *William Morrow*

28 DESIGN FIRM: *Carin Goldberg Design*   DESIGNER: *Carin Goldberg*   HEADLINE TYPEFACE: *Futura*   TEXT TYPEFACE: *Eagle Bold*   CLIENT: *Grove/Atlantic*

29 DESIGN FIRM: *Carin Goldberg Design*   DESIGNER: *Carin Goldberg*   LETTERER: *Gund Larsen*   HEADLINE TYPEFACE: *Zinco*   CLIENT: *Hyperion*

**30 DESIGN FIRM:** *Carin Goldberg Design* **DESIGNER:** *Carin Goldberg* **LETTERER:** *Neil Flewellen* **HEADLINE TYPEFACE:** *Teutonia Zenotype (Redesigned)* **TEXT TYPEFACE:** *Futura* **CLIENT:** *Grove/Atlantic*

**31 DESIGN FIRM:** *Frankfurt Balkind Partners* **DESIGNER:** *Andreas Combuchen and Matt Rollins* **HEADLINE & TEXT TYPEFACE:** *Helvetica Neue Medium and Light* **CLIENT:** *QVC Network, Inc.*

**32 DESIGN FIRM:** *Frankfurt Balkind Partners* **DESIGNER:** *Andreas Combuchen and Matt Rollins* **HEADLINE & TEXT TYPEFACE:** *Helvetica Neue Medium and Light* **CLIENT:** *QVC Network, Inc.*

**30**

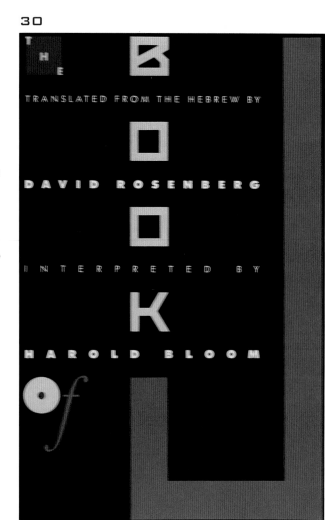

THE BOOK

TRANSLATED FROM THE HEBREW BY

DAVID ROSENBERG

INTERPRETED BY

HAROLD BLOOM

of

**31**

QVC is

1-800-345-1515

annual report 1992

**32**

"In the eight years that my wife and I have been married, this is the first time I have been able to give her a gift that brought tears to her eyes."

– David Kuhlman in St. Louis, Missouri, a QVC shopper for three years.

Diamonique Solitaire 14K Gold Ring, 3 Carats
J5770
QVC Price $108.50

**Carloads of carats**

2,469,280 carats of Diamonique stones were sold to QVC customers last year.

call 1-800-345-1515

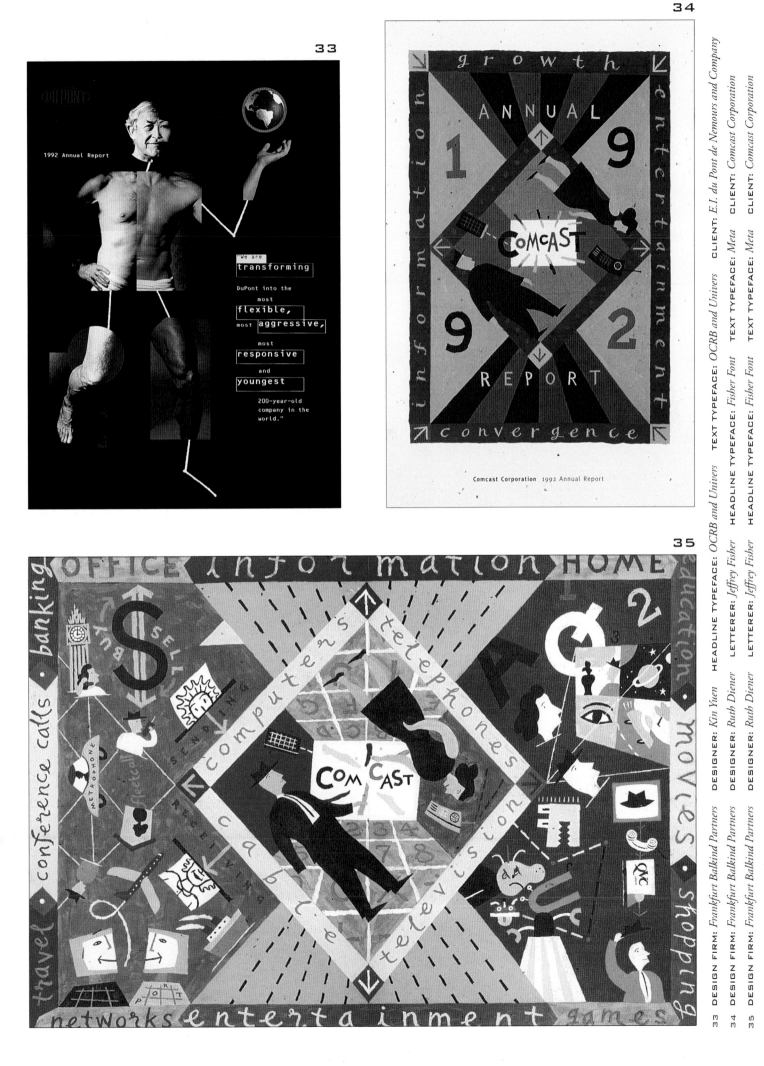

**33**

*1992 Annual Report*

"We are
**transforming**
DuPont into the
most
**flexible,**
most **aggressive,**
most
**responsive**
and
**youngest**
200-year-old
company in the
world."

**34**

Comcast Corporation 1992 Annual Report

**35**

33  DESIGN FIRM: *Frankfurt Balkind Partners*    DESIGNER: *Kin Yuen*    HEADLINE TYPEFACE: OCRB and Univers    TEXT TYPEFACE: OCRB and Univers    CLIENT: *E.I. du Pont de Nemours and Company*

34  DESIGN FIRM: *Frankfurt Balkind Partners*    DESIGNER: *Ruth Diener*    LETTERER: *Jeffrey Fisher*    HEADLINE TYPEFACE: *Fisher Font*    TEXT TYPEFACE: *Meta*    CLIENT: *Comcast Corporation*

35  DESIGN FIRM: *Frankfurt Balkind Partners*    DESIGNER: *Ruth Diener*    LETTERER: *Jeffrey Fisher*    HEADLINE TYPEFACE: *Fisher Font*    TEXT TYPEFACE: *Meta*    CLIENT: *Comcast Corporation*

**36**

**37**

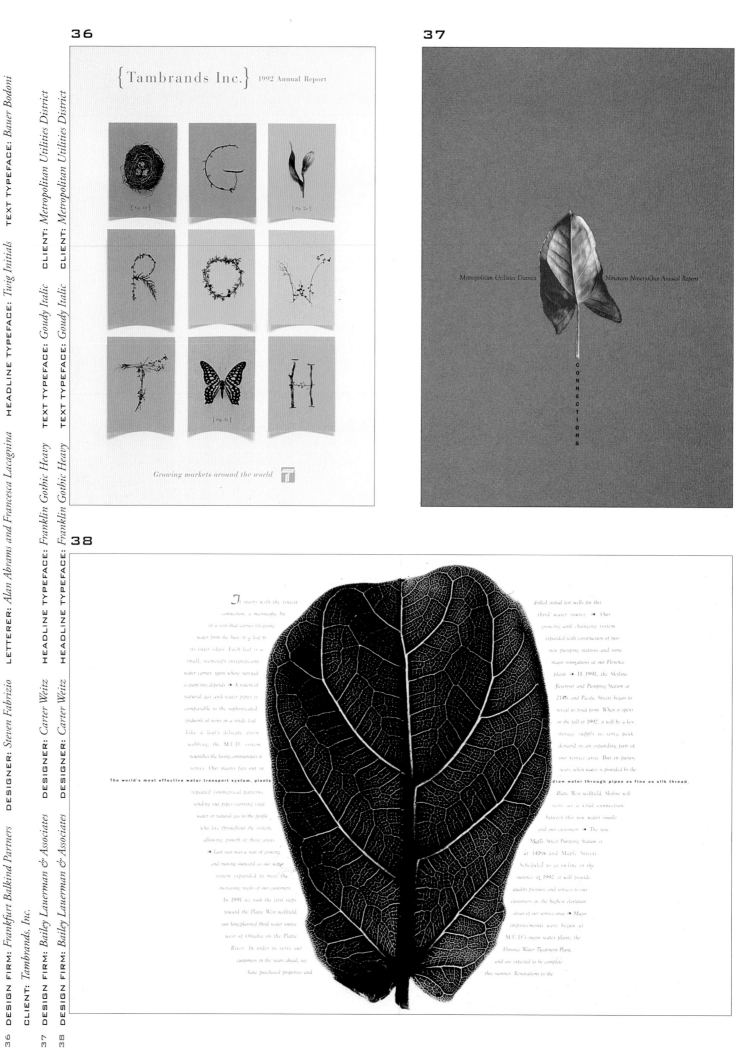

**38**

TEXT TYPEFACE: *Bauer Bodoni*

HEADLINE TYPEFACE: *Twig Initials*

LETTERER: *Alan Abrams and Francesca Lacagnina*

DESIGNER: *Steven Fabrizio*

DESIGN FIRM: *Frankfurt Balkind Partners*

CLIENT: *Tambrands, Inc.*

CLIENT: *Metropolitan Utilities District*

TEXT TYPEFACE: *Goudy Italic*

HEADLINE TYPEFACE: *Franklin Gothic Heavy*

DESIGNER: *Carter Weitz*

DESIGN FIRM: *Bailey Lauerman & Associates*

CLIENT: *Metropolitan Utilities District*

TEXT TYPEFACE: *Goudy Italic*

HEADLINE TYPEFACE: *Franklin Gothic Heavy*

DESIGNER: *Carter Weitz*

DESIGN FIRM: *Bailey Lauerman & Associates*

36  DESIGN FIRM: *Frankfurt Balkind Partners*  DESIGNER: *Steven Fabrizio*  LETTERER: *Alan Abrams and Francesca Lacagnina*  HEADLINE TYPEFACE: *Twig Initials*  TEXT TYPEFACE: *Bauer Bodoni*

CLIENT: *Tambrands, Inc.*

37  DESIGN FIRM: *Bailey Lauerman & Associates*  DESIGNER: *Carter Weitz*  HEADLINE TYPEFACE: *Franklin Gothic Heavy*  TEXT TYPEFACE: *Goudy Italic*  CLIENT: *Metropolitan Utilities District*

38  DESIGN FIRM: *Bailey Lauerman & Associates*  DESIGNER: *Carter Weitz*  HEADLINE TYPEFACE: *Franklin Gothic Heavy*  TEXT TYPEFACE: *Goudy Italic*  CLIENT: *Metropolitan Utilities District*

39

40

39   DESIGN FIRM: *Salsgiver Coveney Assoc. Inc.*   DESIGNER: *Karen Salsgiver and Cathleen Mitchell*   HEADLINE TYPEFACE: *Bernhard Tango and Metro*   TEXT TYPEFACE: *Garamond 3*   CLIENT: *The Juilliard School*

40   DESIGN FIRM: *A Design Collaborative*   DESIGNER: *Dave Mason*   HEADLINE TYPEFACE: *Frutiger*   TEXT TYPEFACE: *Garamond and News Gothic*   CLIENT: *BC TEL*

41

42

43

41 DESIGN FIRM: *Peterson & Company* DESIGNER: *Bryan L. Peterson* HEADLINE TYPEFACE: *Mekanik* TEXT TYPEFACE: *Berkeley Italic* CLIENT: *Mothers Against Drunk Driving*

42 DESIGN FIRM: *Peterson & Company* DESIGNER: *Bryan L. Peterson* HEADLINE TYPEFACE: *Mekanik* TEXT TYPEFACE: *Berkeley Italic* CLIENT: *Mothers Against Drunk Driving*

43 DESIGN FIRM: *Hornall Anderson Design Works* DESIGNER: *Heidi Hatlestad, John Hornall and Julia LaPine* HEADLINE TYPEFACE: *Futura* TEXT TYPEFACE: *Weiss* CLIENT: *Airborne Express*

44

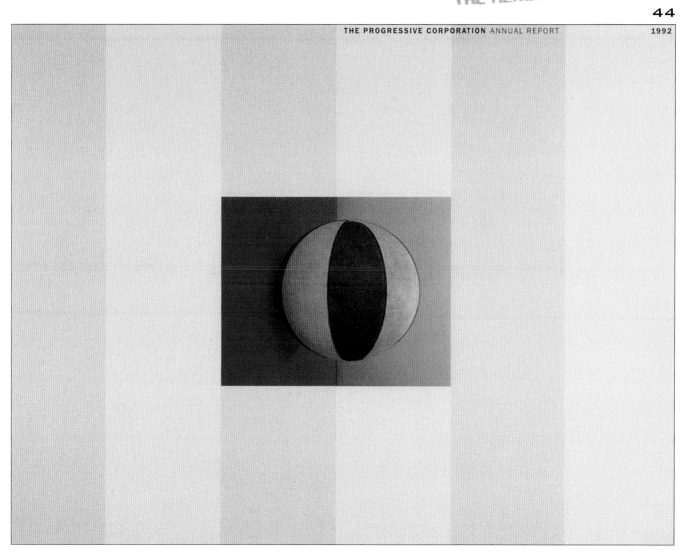

45

Letter to Shareholders

**Progressive's Best Year Ever.** 1992 was a year in which the auto insurance industry faced extraordinary pressures and unprecedented change. In 1992, Progressive continued to implement our simple but radical strategy for reducing the economic costs and human trauma of auto accidents: listen carefully to what consumers are saying, then make the tough decisions necessary to deliver what they want and need. This strategy is transforming the way Progressive does business, and these changes have sometimes been difficult and controversial. I am exceedingly proud to report our highest ever operating profit and revenues, earnings per share and stock price, as well as dramatic improvement in the value our customers receive for the premiums they pay us. In 1992, we again outperformed the industry by a wide margin on return on shareholders' equity, underwriting profit and growth. Approximately 770,000 automobile owners and operators in the United States chose Progressive as their insurance company during 1992 — more than ever before. We plan to further expand our current share of the $90 billion market for personal auto insurance by being the company consumers respect and trust. **Progressive's Customer-Driven Strategy** Auto insurance is at a crossroads. If auto insurance companies fail to accept responsibility for how we do business and are insensitive to our customers' needs, consumers will be driven in desperation to follow the call of consumer activists for more regulation and legislation. The primary example has been California's Proposition 103, an administrative and legal nightmare that has benefited very few consumers. If incentives to compete for and serve customers better are regulated out of existence, the result will be declining insurer financial stability, shrinking availability as insurers continue to pull back from personal auto and deteriorating customer service. →California voters' passage of Proposition 103 has profoundly affected Progressive. Although it disrupted our California business, it has led us to address consumers' mistrust of and dislike for insurance companies by overhauling our business strategy. We are focused on reducing costs, improving service and giving consumers more control over their insurance purchase. →During 1992, we worked hard to improve the auto insurance experience for our customers. •We reduced our loss adjustment and underwriting expenses 9% through quality process improvements and staff reductions. We ended 1992 with 5,591 employees, 19% fewer than at year-end 1991, despite volume growing 10%. Due to 1992 severance payments, we will not see the full financial impact of staff reductions on expenses until 1993. •We reduced auto premium rates for Progressive customers in seven states. In early 1993, we reduced premium rates in four more states. Because these reductions were driven by expense cuts and process improvements, we continue to improve the quality of customer service and to meet our underwriting profit goals. •We improved the speed and empathy of our claim service.

44   DESIGN FIRM: Nesnadny + Schwartz   DESIGNER: Joyce Nesnadny and Michelle Moehler   HEADLINE TYPEFACE: Franklin Gothic   TEXT TYPEFACE: Joanna   CLIENT: The Progressive Corporation

45   DESIGN FIRM: Nesnadny + Schwartz   DESIGNER: Joyce Nesnadny and Michelle Moehler   HEADLINE TYPEFACE: Franklin Gothic   TEXT TYPEFACE: Joanna   CLIENT: The Progressive Corporation

**46**

DILLON

READ

ANNUAL
REVIEW

1991

**47**

WBEZ 91.5 FM
Fiscal 1991 Annual Report

**48**

WBEZ expanded its operation to include a broader range of educational programming in 1971.

Like most public radio stations, WBEZ began as an institutionally licensed station. But institutions such as the Chicago Board of Education became increasingly unable to fund these stations as they were facing their own financial difficulties. Although committed to public radio in Chicago, the Board of Education realized that it could not continue to fund the station, and moved the station toward financial independence by working with a community-based board of directors to oversee the station and administer its license. Special thanks and mention must be given to Kay W

McCurdy, Partner, Lord, Bissell & Brook, who, along with Allan J. Arlow, was crucial in initializing the formation of The WBEZ Alliance, Inc.

On September 19, 1990, WBEZ received its license from the FCC as The WBEZ Alliance, Inc. The board then laid the foundation for the success of the newly independent station. The fine efforts of Edward Grant, Partner, Arthur Andersen & Co., in forging a financial structure for WBEZ were critical in order to secure an efficient fiscal design for the new station's future growth.

A major financial boost came in the form of a $250,000 capital

Victoria Leacman
Co-Host
Artistic Layout

46   DESIGN FIRM: *The Graphic Expression, Inc.*   DESIGNER: *Steve Ferrari*   HEADLINE TYPEFACE: *Gill Sans*   TEXT TYPEFACE: *Sabon*   CLIENT: *Dillon, Read & Co., Inc.*

47   DESIGN FIRM: *Kym Abrams Design*   DESIGNER: *Kym Abrams*   HEADLINE TYPEFACE: *Bauer Bodoni*   TEXT TYPEFACE: *Bauer Bodoni*   CLIENT: *WBEZ 91.5 FM Public Radio Station*

48   DESIGN FIRM: *Kym Abrams Design*   DESIGNER: *Kym Abrams*   HEADLINE TYPEFACE: *Bauer Bodoni*   TEXT TYPEFACE: *Bauer Bodoni*   CLIENT: *WBEZ 91.5 FM Public Radio Station*

49   **DESIGN FIRM:** *Concrete Design Communications Inc.*   **DESIGNER:** *Diti Katona*   **HEADLINE TYPEFACE:** *Bembo*   **TEXT TYPEFACE:** *Bembo*   **CLIENT:** *The First Mercantile Currency Fund*

50   **DESIGN FIRM:** *Hornall Anderson Design Works*   **DESIGNER:** *Jack Anderson, Julie Tanagi-Lock, Lian Ng and John Anicker*   **HEADLINE TYPEFACE:** *Eras*   **TEXT TYPEFACE:** *Sabon*   **CLIENT:** *Starbucks Coffee Co.*

51    **DESIGN FIRM:** *Morla Design*    **DESIGNER:** *Jennifer Morla and Sharrie Brooks*    **HEADLINE TYPEFACE:** *Univers 55, 65 and 75*    **TEXT TYPEFACE:** *Bodoni Book*    **CLIENT:** *SF Airports Commission*

52    **DESIGN FIRM:** *Vaughn Wedeen Creative*    **DESIGNER:** *Steve Wedeen and Lisa Graff*    **HEADLINE TYPEFACE:** *Linoscript and Senator Ultra*    **TEXT TYPEFACE:** *Bernhard*    **CLIENT:** *U.S. West Foundation*

## 51

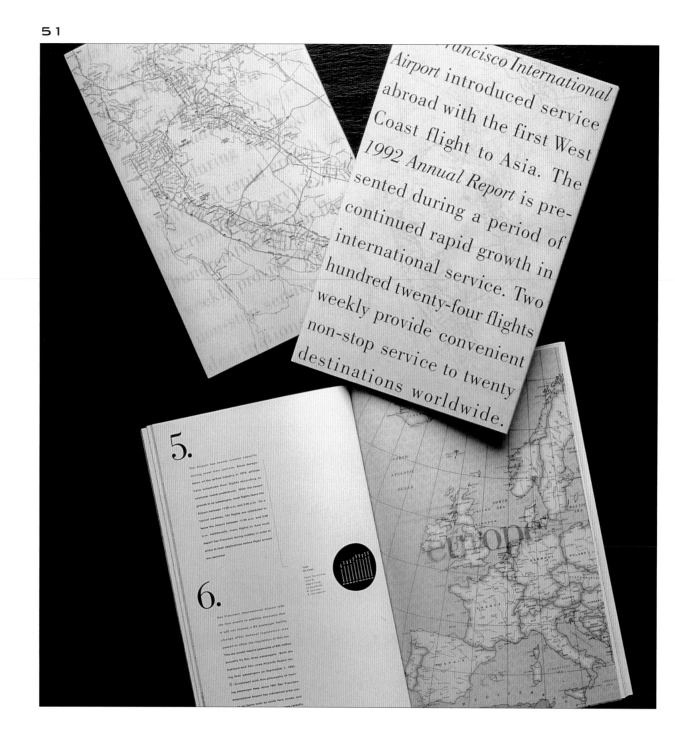

…ancisco International Airport introduced service abroad with the first West Coast flight to Asia. The 1992 Annual Report is presented during a period of continued rapid growth in international service. Two hundred twenty-four flights weekly provide convenient non-stop service to twenty destinations worldwide.

## 52

Independence defines the spirit and heritage of the West: the drive to explore possibilities, pursue new ideas and build self-reliance. The strength of our economic future depends on tapping that spirit, harnessing the talents, imagination and energy of its residents. The U S WEST Foundation's Economic Independence Initiative committed $3.9 million to that quest throughout 1990 and 1991, focusing on three major goals: improving rural economic vitality, promoting the viability of nonprofit organizations and developing outstanding leadership.

**ECONOMIC INDEPENDENCE INITIATIVE**

## 53

The U S WEST Foundation Review for 1990-1991

53 DESIGN FIRM: *Vaughn Wedeen Creative*   DESIGNER: *Steve Wedeen and Lisa Graff*   HEADLINE TYPEFACE: *Linoscript and Senator Ultra*   TEXT TYPEFACE: *Bernhard*   CLIENT: *U.S. West Foundation*

**54** DESIGN FIRM: *Samata Associates* DESIGNER: *Pat and Greg Samata* HEADLINE TYPEFACE: *Univers Thin Ultra Condensed* TEXT TYPEFACE: *Garamond 3 and Univers 75 Black* CLIENT: *HMO America, Inc.*

**55** DESIGN FIRM: *The Graphic Expression, Inc.* DESIGNER: *John Ball* HEADLINE TYPEFACE: *Bodoni* TEXT TYPEFACE: *Bodoni* CLIENT: *Comsat Corp.*

54

We have adopted a flexible benefits plan. The employee has some choice of benefits, and pays some of the cost. Therefore, both the employee and company are looking for value and service. Managed care plans can offer a different level of accountability than do many indemnity insurance programs. With the facility to call upon a convenient and independent review to resolve problems without interfering with the employer/employee relationship, such managed care plans can deliver and be accountable for high quality medical care to the individual.

**JIM GOSE**

*Corporate Human Resources,*

*Underwriters Laboratory*

55

Our job is to find where we're strongest and cultivate those strengths. Video is another example. Fiber optics are tied to fixed points, so they can't serve multiple distribution points like the ones that video systems have. We can. And in 1992, we'll launch a satellite dedicated exclusively to video.

New competitors will keep us on our toes. Recent FCC rulings have opened to competition the U.S. market for private communications networks used by multinational corporations. It will be good for us. And keep in mind that we already provide reliable service to 110 nations. It will be a long time before any other system can match that reach.

## Which business is growing the fastest?

COMSAT Mobile Communications has been a smashing success. For one thing, it's not susceptible to competition from fiber optic communications — you can't tie a cable to a ship or a plane. And it's vertically integrated. That means we go right to the end customer, and we add value that competitors have a very tough time matching.

We're seeing explosive new growth in all mobile areas — maritime, aeronautical and land mobile. International communications is growing dramatically. Name another industry that's getting sustainable double-digit results in a recession. You can't.

## How is COMSAT World Systems performing?

COMSAT World Systems had a wonderful year. Very strong, performing up to all expectations. Our strategy is to extend our long-term contracts, add as much value as we can, provide as many new services as we can and maintain our current position as the dominant force in the market.

**VOICE GRADE CIRCUITS**

57

56

LINCOLN NATIONAL CORPORATION

ANNUAL REPORT 1991

ICOS Corporation 1992 Annual Report

icos

58

56  **DESIGN FIRM:** *Samata Associates*  **DESIGNER:** *Greg Samata*  **HEADLINE TYPEFACE:** *Caslon Openface*  **TEXT TYPEFACE:** *Copperplate 32 BC*  **CLIENT:** *Lincoln National Corporation*

57  **DESIGN FIRM:** *Van Dyke Company*  **DESIGNER:** *John Van Dyke and Ann Kumasaka*  **HEADLINE TYPEFACE:** *OCR-B*  **TEXT TYPEFACE:** *Janson Text Roman and Italic*  **CLIENT:** *ICOS Corporation*

58  **DESIGN FIRM:** *Samata Associates*  **DESIGNER:** *Pat Samata*  **HEADLINE TYPEFACE:** *Courier*  **TEXT TYPEFACE:** *Copperplate 33 BC, Univers 85 Extra Black, Caslon 3, Caslon 540, Courier, Univers 57 and 67*

**CLIENT:** *YMCA of Metropolitan Chicago*

**59**

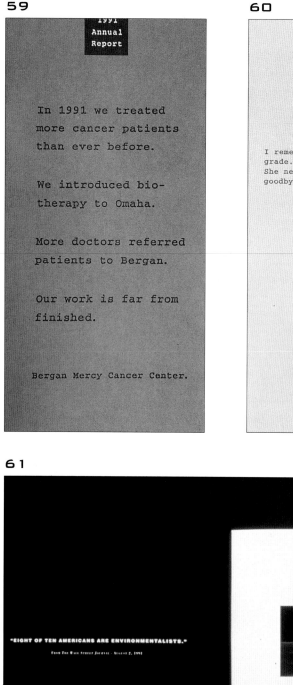

1991 Annual Report

In 1991 we treated more cancer patients than ever before.

We introduced bio-therapy to Omaha.

More doctors referred patients to Bergan.

Our work is far from finished.

Bergan Mercy Cancer Center.

**60**

patients with the best possible care available. Because of the wide variety of malignancies we treated and our continuing education, we improved our medical treatment knowledge and patient services. Ours is a team with great dedication, utilizing every means available in the fight against this dreaded disease.

I remember when I was in fifth grade. My teacher just left one day. She never came back. She never said goodbye.

He was honest with his students about his illness. He didn't go into detail about the cancer but let them know that when they returned from spring break he may look different.

In Georgia, 1988, Jim was diagnosed with an ocular melanoma which required an enucleation of the eye. He thought that was it, until he went for a routine physical in March of 1991 in Omaha. His physician told him his blood work results had come back abnormal and that further testing needed to be done. After X-rays and a biopsy, Jim was diagnosed with liver metastasis from his ocular melanoma.

He was then introduced to 5 South, the dedicated oncology unit at Bergan Mercy Medical Center. A place with people he believes to be part of his family and he also believes their care and attitude is a big reason why he is still alive today. "They let me be in control of my life. They didn't just come in and

8

**61**

"EIGHT OF TEN AMERICANS ARE ENVIRONMENTALISTS."

FROM THE WALL STREET JOURNAL – AUGUST 2, 1991

THE PARADOX OF PROGRESS

THE ENVIRONMENTAL PROTECTION A[...]

FEDERALLY REGULATED POLLUTIO[...]

FUELS POLLUTION, THE TENDENCY'S B[...]

AGAINST PROGRESS.                    ONE OR T[...]

IRONICALLY, AIDING          THE ENVIRONMENT

SPAWNED GROWTH:          $100 BILLION A YEAR

IN ENVIRONMENTAL SERVICES. WHILE THIS DOES NOT MEAN THAT $1

SPENT ON THE ENVIRONMENT EQUALS $1 IN EXPANSION, IT SHOWS

THAT THE SOLUTION LIES WITHIN THE PROBLEM. THAT'S PROGRESS.

59 DESIGN FIRM: *Bailey Lauerman & Associates*  DESIGNER: *Shelley Hanna*  HEADLINE TYPEFACE: *Courier*  TEXT TYPEFACE: *Courier*  CLIENT: *Bailey Lauerman & Associates*

60 DESIGN FIRM: *Bailey Lauerman & Associates*  DESIGNER: *Shelley Hanna*  HEADLINE TYPEFACE: *Courier*  TEXT TYPEFACE: *Courier*  CLIENT: *Bailey Lauerman & Associates*

61 DESIGN FIRM: *Rigsby Design, Inc.*  DESIGNER: *Lana Rigsby and Troy S. Ford*  HEADLINE TYPEFACE: *Helvetica Black*  TEXT TYPEFACE: *Bodoni*  CLIENT: *The Earth Technology Corp.*

62

63

64

65  DESIGN FIRM: *Plunkett + Kuhr*   DESIGNER: *John Plunkett and Barbara Kuhr*   HEADLINE TYPEFACE: *Adobe Myriad*   TEXT TYPEFACE: *Adobe Myriad*   CLIENT: *Wired Magazine*

66  DESIGN FIRM: *Plunkett + Kuhr*   DESIGNER: *John Plunkett and Barbara Kuhr*   HEADLINE TYPEFACE: *Adobe Myriad and Waldbaum Book*   TEXT TYPEFACE: *Adobe Myriad*   CLIENT: *Wired Magazine*

**65**

**66**

68

67 DESIGN FIRM: Zone Studios/After Hours   DESIGNER: Brian Stauffer and Todd Ferell   CLIENT: Zone Publications   Bryan . Peterson   CLIENT: Zone Publications

68 DESIGN FIRM: Emphasis (Hong Kong) Ltd.   DESIGNER: Percy Chung   LETTERER: Percy Chung   DESIGNER: Percy Chung   CLIENT: Cathay Pacific Airlines

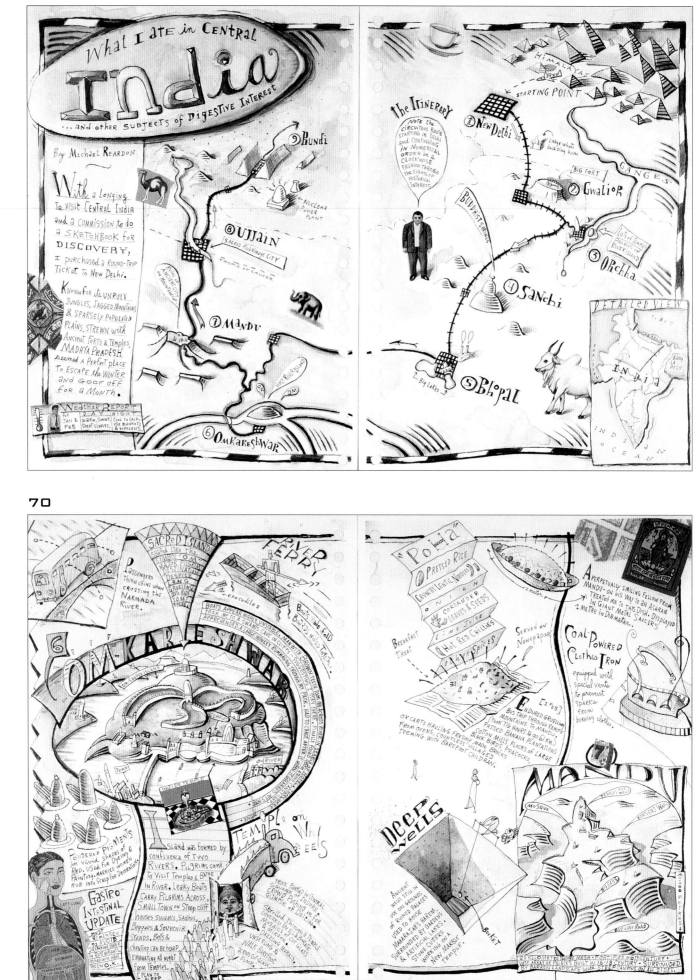

69    DESIGN FIRM: *Emphasis (Hong Kong) Ltd.*    DESIGNER: *Michael Reardon*    LETTERER: *Michael Reardon*    CLIENT: *Cathay Pacific Airlines*

70    DESIGN FIRM: *Emphasis (Hong Kong) Ltd.*    DESIGNER: *Michael Reardon*    LETTERER: *Michael Reardon*    CLIENT: *Cathay Pacific Airlines*

**71 DESIGN FIRM:** *Kutztown University* **DESIGNER:** *Elaine J. Steinger and Amy Lapides* **HEADLINE TYPEFACE:** *ITC Garamond* **TEXT TYPEFACE:** *Gill Sans* **CLIENT:** *Kutztown University*

## 72

**NEW NICHE FOR**

# Nash

Setting up a fine art photographic printing operation isn't a common career move for a world-famous rock musician. Yet to Graham Nash, it offered an obvious path leading from his lifetime's interest in photography. No darkroom operation this: Nash Editions uses giant ink-jet printers to produce images on surfaces that were once thought impossible. Simon Eccles met him in a Cologne coffee bar

## 73

Photograph by The Douglas Brothers

## DESCENDANTS.

The Descendants of a Movie-Going Republic

Alexander Chee, author of "The Descendants of a Movie-Going Republic," is a writer living in Iowa City, Iowa, where he is at work on his first novel, *Saint Spencer of the Loft.*

72  DESIGN FIRM: XYZ Magazine   DESIGNER: Wayne Ford   HEADLINE TYPEFACE: SH Futura Extrabold   TEXT TYPEFACE: Futura Light   CLIENT: XYZ Magazine   TEXT TYPEFACE: Franklin Gothic Bold and Light

73  DESIGN FIRM: Pentagram Design Ltd.   DESIGNER: Vince Frost   LETTERER: Vince Frost   HEADLINE TYPEFACE: Various Original Wood Types

CLIENT: Big Magazine

74  **DESIGN FIRM:** Segura Inc.    **DESIGNER:** Carlos Segura    **HEADLINE TYPEFACE:** Centenial    **TEXT TYPEFACE:** Centenial    **CLIENT:** PUSH!

75  **DESIGN FIRM:** Adobe Systems Inc.    **DESIGNER:** Laurie Szujewska, James Young and Margery Cantor    **HEADLINE TYPEFACE:** Minion Multiple Master    **TEXT TYPEFACE:** Minion Multiple Master    **CLIENT:** Minion Multiple Master

    **CLIENT:** Adobe Systems Inc.

76  **DESIGN FIRM:** Lloyd Ziff Design Group, Inc.    **DESIGNER:** Lloyd Ziff    **TEXT TYPEFACE:** Galliard    **CLIENT:** LuluBelle's Restaurant

MISCELLANEOUS

1   DESIGN FIRM: *Jager DiPaola Kemp Design*   DESIGNER: *Janet Johnson*   HEADLINE TYPEFACE: *Courier*   TEXT TYPEFACE: *Bank Gothic*   CLIENT: *Queen City Printers*

2   DESIGN FIRM: *Muller + Company*   DESIGNER: *John Muller*   HEADLINE TYPEFACE: *Empire and Park Avenue*   CLIENT: *Spangler*

3   DESIGN FIRM: *Ema Design*   DESIGNER: *Debra Johnson Humphrey*   HEADLINE TYPEFACE: *Garamond No. 3 Italic*   TEXT TYPEFACE: *Garamond No. 3 Italic*   CLIENT: *James Gritz*

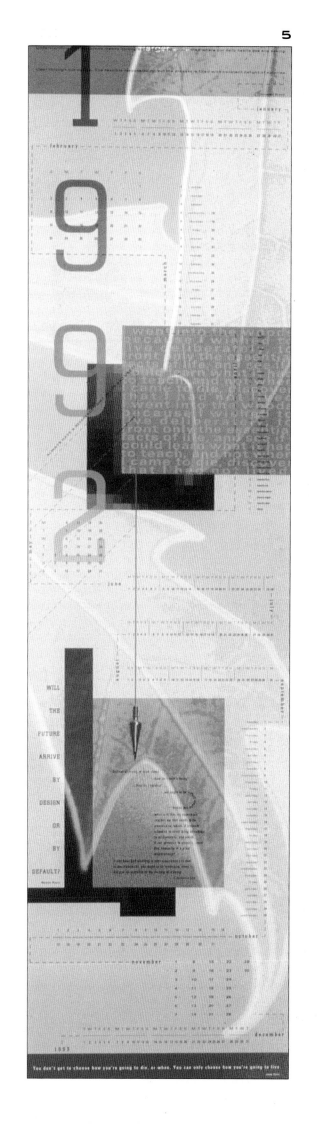

**DESIGN FIRM:** *George Tscherny, Inc.*    **DESIGNER:** *George Tscherny*    **LETTERER:** *George Tscherny, Beth Laub and Michelle Novak*    **TEXT TYPEFACE:** *Walbaum*    **CLIENT:** *SEI Corporation*

**DESIGN FIRM:** *Tara Carson Design*    **DESIGNER:** *Tara Carson*    **HEADLINE TYPEFACE:** *City*    **TEXT TYPEFACE:** *Univers*    **CLIENT:** *Tara Carson Design*

4    DESIGN FIRM: *George Tscherny, Inc.*

5    DESIGN FIRM: *Tara Carson Design*

**6**

**7**

**8**

Wishing you
good fortune
and good health
in the year ahead.

PAUL SHAW LETTER DESIGN & PETER KRUTY EDITIONS

HAPPY
B-DAY

6  **DESIGN FIRM:** Landor Associates  **DESIGNER:** Margaret Youngblood and Rachel O'Dowd  **CLIENT:** Bay Area Discovery Museum  **HEADLINE TYPEFACE:** Bodoni  **TEXT TYPEFACE:** Handlettering

7  **DESIGN FIRM:** Hallmark Cards, Inc.  **DESIGNER:** Barbi Loesing  **LETTERER:** Barbi Loesing  **CLIENT:** Hallmark Cards, Inc.

8  **DESIGN FIRM:** Paul Shaw/Letter Design  **DESIGNER:** Paul Shaw  **LETTERER:** Paul Shaw  **CLIENT:** Paul Shaw/Letter Design and Peter Kruty Editions

11

12

9   DESIGN FIRM: *Zimmermann Crowe Design*    DESIGNER: *Rudiger Gotz*    CLIENT: *Zimmermann Crowe Design*    LETTERER: *Rudiger Gotz*    TEXT TYPEFACE: *Meta*    HEADLINE TYPEFACE: *Meta*

10   DESIGN FIRM: *Schmeltz + Warren*    DESIGNER: *Crit Warren*    CLIENT: *Columbus Society of Communicating Arts*    TEXT TYPEFACE: *Handlettering*    HEADLINE TYPEFACE: *Handlettering*

11   DESIGN FIRM: *Tim Girvin Design, Inc.*    DESIGNER: *Tim Girvin*    LETTERER: *Tim Girvin*    CLIENT: *Manpower Inc.*    TEXT TYPEFACE: *Handlettering*    HEADLINE TYPEFACE: *Handlettering*

12   DESIGN FIRM: *Rigsby Design, Inc.*    DESIGNER: *Lana Rigsby*    LETTERER: *Lana Rigsby*    CLIENT: *ZOOT Restaurant*    TEXT TYPEFACE: *Futura Book and Extrabold*

13

TALISMAN

WARD
AWAY
EVIL

SHELTER
RESIDENTS'
UNIQUE
SYMBOL
FORM

THEIR
SPECIAL
CODE

14

15

13 DESIGN FIRM: BJ Krivanek Art + Design    DESIGNER: Joel Breaux    CLIENT: Children of the Night – Los Angeles, CA    HEADLINE TYPEFACE: Handlettering    CLIENT: Levi Strauss & Co.

14 DESIGN FIRM: Zimmermann Crowe Design    LETTERER: Alan Disparte    DESIGNER: Alan Disparte

15 DESIGN FIRM: Weber Design Partners    DESIGNER: Christina Weber and David Wise    TEXT TYPEFACE: Bembo Italic and Gill Sans    CLIENT: Art in the Streets Community Project

16 DESIGN FIRM: *Primo Angeli Inc.*    DESIGNER: *Philippe Becker*    LETTERER: *Terrence Tong, Philippe Becker and Phil Ting*    HEADLINE TYPEFACE: *Handlettering*    TEXT TYPEFACE: *News Gothic*

CLIENT: *U.S. Postal Service*

**17**

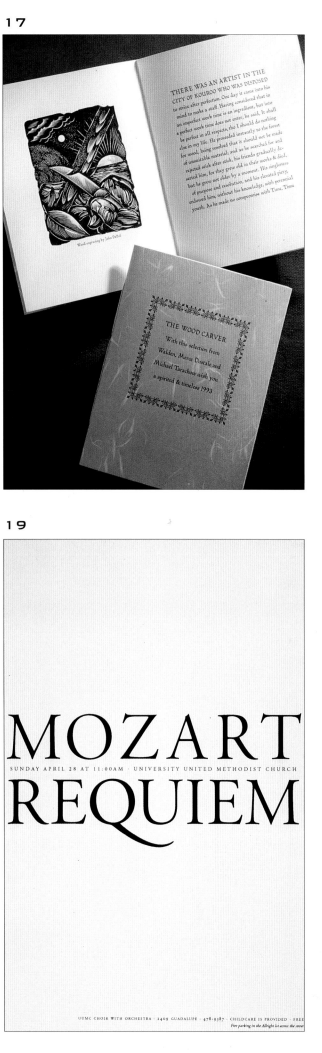

**18**

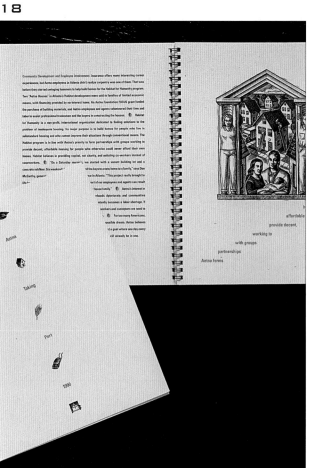

**19**

MOZART
REQUIEM

SUNDAY APRIL 28 AT 11:00AM · UNIVERSITY UNITED METHODIST CHURCH

UUMC CHOIR WITH ORCHESTRA · 2409 GUADALUPE · 478-9387 · CHILDCARE IS PROVIDED · FREE
*Free parking in the Allright lot across the street*

**20**

17  DESIGN FIRM: *Pentagram Press*  DESIGNER: *Michael Tarachow*  HEADLINE TYPEFACE: *Verona, handset*  TEXT TYPEFACE: *Verona, handset*  CLIENT: *Pentagram Press*

18  DESIGN FIRM: *Aetna*  DESIGNER: *Lee Faragosa*  HEADLINE TYPEFACE: *Univers 67*  TEXT TYPEFACE: *Univers 67 and Univers 47*  CLIENT: *Aetna*

19  DESIGN FIRM: *Fuller Dyal & Stamper*  DESIGNER: *Herman Dyal*  LETTERER: *Herman Dyal*  HEADLINE TYPEFACE: *Memphis*  TEXT TYPEFACE: *Garamond and Garamond Expert*  CLIENT: *University United Methodist Church*

20  DESIGN FIRM: *Marc English Design*  DESIGNER: *Marc English*  HEADLINE TYPEFACE: *Memphis, Insignia, Industria, Brush Script*  TEXT TYPEFACE: *Memphis*  CLIENT: *Minuteman Council Boy Scouts of America*

22

21  DESIGN FIRM: *Pentagram Press*  DESIGNER: *Michael Tarachow*  HEADLINE TYPEFACE: *Poliphilus and Verona, handset*  TEXT TYPEFACE: *Verona, handset*  CLIENT: *Pentagram Press*

22  DESIGN FIRM: *Aetna Strategic Design Dept.*  DESIGNER: *Anne Allen*  HEADLINE TYPEFACE: *Bodoni*  TEXT TYPEFACE: *Univers*  CLIENT: *Aetna Gallery*

# INDEX

**DESIGN FIRM ADRESSES**

246 Fifth Design
246 Fifth Avenue
Ottawa Ontario KIS2N3
CANADA
613-231-3000

A Design Collaborative
85 Columbia
Seattle, WA 98104
USA
206-621-1235

Adobe Systems, Inc.
1585 Charleston Road
Mountain, CA 94043
USA
415-962-2721

Aetna
151 Farmington Avenue
Hartford, CT 06156
USA
203-273-0123

After Hours
1201 East Jefferson #B100
Phoenix, AZ 85034
USA
602-256-2648

American Express Publishing
1120 Avenue of the Americas
New York, NY 10036
USA
212-382-5729

Axiom Design
359 W. Pierpont Avenue
Salt Lake City, UT 64101
USA
801-432-2442

Bailey Lauerman & Associates
900 NBC Center
Lincoln, NE 68508
USA
402-475-2800

Barker Campbell & Farley
240 Business Park Drive
Virginia Beach, CA 23462
USA
804-497-4811

Bielenberg Design
333 Bryant Street #130
San Francisco, CA 94107
USA
415-495-3371

Brad Norr Design
126 North Third Street #404
Minneapolis, MN 55401
USA
612-339-2104

Bruce Hale Design Studio
1201 N.W. Blakely Court
Seattle, WA 98117
USA
206-440-9036

Bruce Yelaska Design
1546 Grant Avenue
San Francisco, CA 94133
USA
415-392-0717

Carin Goldberg Design
One University Place
New York, NY 10003
USA
212-674-6424

Carol Publishing Group
600 Madison Avenue 11th Floor
New York, NY 10022
USA
212-418-4067

Cipriani Kremer Design
2 Copley Place
Boston, MA 02116
USA
617-236-1422

Clifford Selbert Design, Inc.
2067 Massachusetts Avenue
Cambridge, MA 02140
USA
617-497-6605

Concrete Design
Communications, Inc.
2 Silver Avenue
Toronto, Ontario M6R3A2
Canada
416-534-9960

Dayton Hudson Marshall Fields
700 On The Mall Box 100
Minneapolis, MN 55401
USA
612-375-3995

DBD International, Ltd.
38 Park Avenue
Rutherford, NJ 07070
USA
201-896-8476

Design/Art Inc.
6311 Romaine Street #7311
Los Angeles, CA 90038
USA
213-467-2984

Drenttel Doyle Partners
1123 Broadway
New York, NY 10010
USA
212-463-8787

Ema Design
1228 15th Street Ste. #301
Denver, CO 80202
USA
303-835-0222

Emerson, Wajdowicz Studios, Inc.
1123 Broadway
New York, NY 10010
USA
212-807-8144

Evenson Design Group
4445 Overland Avenue
Culver City, CA 90203
USA
310-204-1995

Eye Cue Design
1670 Yosemite Avenue #103
Sun Valley, CA 93063
USA
805-527-1338

Fiorentino Associates
134 W. 26th St. #902
New York, NY 10001
USA
212-421-5888

Fuller Dyal & Stamper
1711 S. Congress Ste. #300
Austin, TX 78704
USA
512-447-7733

Gardner Design
100 North 6th St.
#901-A
Minneapolis, MN 55403
USA
612-332-2270

George Tscherny
238 East 72nd Street
New York, NY 10021
USA
212-734-3277

Gerard Huerta Design, Inc.
54 Old Post Road
Southport, CT 06490
USA
203-256-1625

Grady, Campbell, Inc.
920 N. Franklin Ste. #404
Chicago, IL 60610
USA
312-642-6511

Graphics & Designing, Inc.
203 Shiroganedaisun Plaza 5-18-9
Shiroganedai 108
Minato-Ku Tokyo
Japan
03-3449-0651

Graphiculture
332 1st Avenue North
Ste.#304
Minneapolis, MN 55401
USA
612-239-8271

Hallmark Cards, Inc.
25th & McGee
Kansas City, MO 64141
USA
816-274-8175

Henry Holt & Co.
115 W. 18th Street
New York, NY 10011
USA
212-886-9524

Hornall Anderson Design Works
1008 Western Avenue Ste. 600
Seattle, WA 98104
USA
206-467-5800

I.F. Planning, Inc.
1-1-18 Kitahama Chuo-Ku
Osaka 541
Japan
06-231-8282

Independent Project Press
PO Box 1033
Sedonia, AZ 86339
USA
602-204-1332

Jager DiPaola Kemp Design
308 Pine Street
Burlington, VT 06501
USA
802-864-5884

Jun Sato Design, Inc.
#13A Metabohankyo 1-5 Tsurunoch
Kitaku Osaka 530
Japan
06-372-5317

Kan-tai-Keung Design & Associates
28/F Great Smart Tower
230 Wanchai Road
Wanchai Hong Kong
852-574-8399

Kutztown University
106 East Main Street
Fleetwood, PA 19522
USA
215-944-0683

Kym Abrams Design
711 S. Dearborn Ste. #205
Chicago, IL 60605
USA
312-341-0709

Landor Associates
1001 Front St.
San Francisco, CA 94111
USA
415-955-1201

Lewis Moberly
33 Greese Street
London W1PIPN
071-580-9252

Lippincott & Margulies Inc.
499 Park Avenue
New York, NY 10022
USA
212-832-3000

Lisa Levin Design
3020 Broadway Ste. #107
Sausalito, CA 94965
USA
415-332-9410

Looking
660 South Avenue 21 #5
Los Angeles, CA 90031
USA
213-227-1450

Lorna Stovale Design
1088 Queen Anne Place
Los Angeles, CA 90019
USA
213-931-5984

M Plus M Inc.
17 Cornelia Street
New York, NY 10014
USA
212-807-0248

Marc English Design
37 Wellington Avenue
Lexington, MA 02173
USA
617-860-0800

Mark Oliver Inc.
1 West Victoria St.
Santa Barbara, CA 93101
USA
805-963-0734

Maureen Erbe Design
1948 S. La Chierega Blvd.
Los Angeles, CA 90034
USA
310-839-1947

Nesnandy + Schwartz
10803 Magnolia Drive
Cleveland, OH 44106
USA
216-791-7721

Michael Schwab Design
80 Liberty Ship Way #7
Sausalito, CA 94965
USA
415-331-7621

Morla Design
463 Bryant Street
San Francisco, CA 94017
USA
415-543-6548

Muller & Co.
4839 Belleview
Kansas, MO 64112
USA
816-531-1992

Musser Design
558 Race Street
Harrisburg, PA 17104
USA
717-233-4411

Newell and Sorrell Ltd.
4 Utopia Village Chalcot Road
London NW18LH
Great Brititan
071-722-1113

Packaging Create Inc.
Daito Bldg. 2F 5-13-11
Nishitemma
Kitaku Osaka 530
Japan
06-312-7978

Pam Cerio Design
7710 Wake Robin Drive
Cleveland, OH 44130
USA
216-845-3055

Parham Santana
7 West 18th Street
New York, NY 10011
USA
212-645-7501

Pat Taylor
3540 South Street NW
Washington, DC
USA
202-338-0962

Patricia Bruning Design
1045 Sansome #219
San Francisco, CA 94111
USA
415-296-0433

Paul Shaw/Letter Design
785 West End Avenue
New York, NY 10025
USA
212-666-3738

Pentagram Design Ltd.
11 Needham Road
London W112RP
England
071-229-3477

Pentagram Press
4925 South Nicollet Avenue
Minneapolis, MN 55409
USA
612-824-4576

Peterson & Co.
2200 N. Lamar Ste. #310
Dallas, TX 75202
USA
214-954-0522

Ph.D
1524 A. Cloverfield Blvd.
Santa Monica, CA 90404
USA
310-829-0900

Pinkhaus Design Corp.
2424 South Dixie Highway
Miami, FL 33133
USA
305-854-1000

Plunkett & Kuhr
PO Box 2237
557 Park Avenue
Park City, UT 84060
USA
801-649-1702

plus design inc.
10 Thatcher Street Ste. #109
Boston, MA 02113
USA
617-367-9587

Powell Street Studio
2135 Powell Street
San Francisco, CA 94133
USA
415-986-6564

Primo Angeli, Inc.
590 Folsom St.
San Francisco, CA 95105
USA
415-974-6100

Rapp Collins Communications
901 Marquette Avenue 17th Floor
Minneapolis, MN 55402
USA
612-373-3046

Richard Poulin Design Group
268 Spring St.
New York, NY 10010
USA
212-675-1332

Rick Jost
229 33rd Avenue East
Seattle, WA 98112
USA
206-325-9601

Rickabaugh Graphics
384 W. Johnston Road
Gahanna, OH 43230
USA
614-337-2229

Rigsby Design Inc.
5640 Kirby Drive Ste. #260
Houston, TX 77005
USA
713-299-3477

Robert Valentine Inc.
17 Vestry Street 2nd Floor
New York, NY 10013
USA
212-925-3103

Runnion Design
755 Salem Street
Lynnfield, MA 01940
USA
617-596-2727

Ryle Smith Studio
6348 Pierce Street
Omaha, NE 68106
USA
402-556-2779

Sackett Design
864 Folsom St.
San Francisco, CA 94107
USA
415-543-1590

Salisbury Communications, Inc.
2200 Amapola Court
Torrance, CA 90501
USA
310-320-7660

Salsgiver Coveney Assoc. Inc.
4 Birch Road
Westport, CT 06880
USA
203-454-1056

Sayles Graphic Design
308 Eighth St.
Des Moines, IA 50309
USA
515-243-2922

Schmeltz & Warren
74 Sheffield Road
Columbus, OH 43214-2514
USA
614-262-3055

Segura Inc.
540 N. Lake Shore Drive #324
Chicago, IL 60611-3431
USA
312-645-1156

Stewart Monderer Design, Inc.
10 Thatcher St. Ste. #12
Boston, MA 02113
USA
617-720-5555

Stolze Design
40 Melcher Street 4th Floor
Boston, MA 02210
USA
617-350-7109

Sullivan Perkins
2811 McKenney Avenue Ste. #320
Dallas, TX
USA
214-922-9080

Tara Carson Design
782 E. California Blvd. #2
Pasadena, CA 91106
USA
818-568-0780

Tatsu Inc.
Uchihonmachi 55 Bldg 303 1-3-10
Uchihonmachi Chuo-Ku 540
Osaka
Japan
06-947-5815

Tharp Did It
50 University Avenue Ste. #21
Los Gatos, CA 90530
USA
408-354-6726

The Graphic Expression
330 East 59th Street
New York, NY 10022
USA
212-759-7788

The Lapis Press
589 N. Venice Blvd.
Venice, CA 90291
USA
310-396-4152

The Leonhardt Group
1218 3rd Avenue #620
Seattle, WA 98101
USA
206-624-0551

The Pushpin Group, Inc.
215 Park Avenue South
New York, NY 1003
USA
212-951-5251

Tim Girvin Design Inc.
1601 2nd Avenue 5th Floor
Seattle, WA 98101
USA
206-623-7808

Tom Fowler Inc.
9 Webbs Hill Road
Stanford, CT 06903
USA
203-329-1105

Tutsell St. John Lambie-Nairn
48 Beak Street
London WIR30A
England
071-753-84676

Van Dyke Co.
85 Columbia
Seattle, WA 98104
USA
206-329-1105

Vaughn Wedeen Creative
407 Rio Grande NW
Albuquerque, NM 87104
USA
505-243-4000

Vickie Karten Design
236 Howland Canal
Venice, CA 90291
USA
310-822-2176

Vincent Lisi
372 Douglas Street
Brooklyn, NY 11217
USA
718-789-4872

Visual Asylum
343 4th Ste. A
San Diego, CA 92010
USA
619-233-9633

Vrontikis Design Office
2021 Pontius Avenue
Los Angeles, CA 90025
USA
310 478-4775

Warner Brothers Records
3300 Warner Blvd.
Burbank, CA 91505
USA
818-953-3364

White Design
4500 E. Pacific Coast Highway
Ste. #320
Long Beach, CA 90804
USA
310-597-7772

Zimmerman Crowe Design
90 Tehama
San Francisco, CA 94105
USA
415-777-5560